GERMAN
GRAMMAR

WITHDRAWN

Authors
**Reinhard Tenberg
and Guido Rings**

Consultant
Duncan Sidwell

Developed by the BBC Language Unit
Edited by Naomi Laredo
Project managed by Stenton Associates
Proofread by Robin Sawers
Produced by **AMR**
Original design by Oxprint Design
Cover artwork by Elaine Cox

© Reinhard Tenberg & Guido Rings 1996

ISBN 0 563 39944 9

Published by BBC Books, a division of BBC Worldwide Ltd
Woodlands, 80 Wood Lane, London W12 0TT
First published 1996

Text and cover printed by Clays Ltd, St Ives Plc

Also available:
    BBC French Grammar
    BBC Italian Grammar
    BBC Spanish Grammar

Introduction

The BBC German Grammar is for adult learners, whether learning at home or on Adult/Further Education or non-specialist Higher Education language courses. It is also ideal for GCSE students.

It is a practical reference book which makes German grammar accessible to English-speaking learners, and it is the ideal complement to any course book. The emphasis is on clear and concise explanation of the core structures of German, illustrated by examples using current, everyday language.

It is not necessary to have a detailed formal knowledge of English grammar to use this book, since the use of technical grammatical terms has been restricted to those which are essential. There is also a glossary to help clarify these terms.

The book is designed to allow easy and rapid consultation. It comprises:

- the list of contents – a quick way to find the section or subsection you want;

- a glossary of grammatical terms;

- grammar explanations clearly laid out in numbered sections and subsections. The first half of the book covers nouns, articles, adjectives, adverbs, pronouns and prepositions. The second half focuses on verbs (formation, use and irregular forms) and sentence structure;

- verb tables – the patterns for regular verbs and for commonly used irregular verbs;

- a fully comprehensive, easy-to-use index, which lists key words in German and English as well as grammatical terms.

Contents

active (see voice)

adjective

An adjective is a word which describes a noun.

*It is a **big** house.*
*The garden is **big**, too.*
*It is **bigger** than our old one.*

In English, the form of the adjective only changes for the comparative (*bigger*) and for the superlative (*biggest*). In German, adjectives which immediately precede a noun change to agree with the gender, number and case of the noun they describe.

adverb

An adverb is a word which adds information about a verb, an adjective or another adverb.

*She spoke **slowly**, but **very clearly**.*
*That's **rather** nice.*

agreement

In German, the form of an adjective (preceding a noun), an article or a pronoun has to 'agree' with the gender, number and (usually) case of the noun or pronoun it accompanies or replaces.

article

There are two types of article in English and German: definite (*the*) and indefinite (*a, an*). However, in German the form of both definite and indefinite articles changes to agree in gender, case and number with the noun to which they refer.

auxiliary verb

An auxiliary verb is used together with another verb when forming compound tenses.

*I **have** failed the examination. I **shall** go to Germany.*

The German auxiliary verbs are **haben, sein** and **werden**.

case
The case of a noun or pronoun indicates its function in the sentence or clause. German has four cases: nominative (for the subject), accusative and dative (for objects and after prepositions) and genitive (expressing possession, for objects and after prepositions).

> *Der Zug kam pünktlich.* (nominative: subject)
> *Wir nehmen den Zug um 8.15 Uhr.* (accusative: direct object)
> *Im (In dem) Zug gab es keinen Speisewagen.* (dative: after preposition)

clause
A clause is a group of words which includes a subject and a verb. It may or may not constitute a complete sentence.

> *I am leaving.* (one clause – one sentence)
> *I am leaving when I've finished.* (two clauses – one sentence)

comparative (see adjective)

conjugation/conjugate
A conjugation is the pattern of a verb's forms. For example, the regular verb *to talk* is conjugated as follows: infinitive *to talk*, present tense *I talk, he/she talks*, past *I talked*, perfect *I have talked*, etc.

conjunction
A conjunction is a word which links single words, phrases or clauses, such as *and, or, but, though, because*.

declension/decline
A declension is the set of endings added to German nouns, articles, pronouns and adjectives to indicate their gender, case and number. For example, the noun *das Buch* is declined as follows: nominative/accusative

singular *das Buch*, genitive singular *des Buch(e)s*,
nominative/accusative plural *die Bücher*, etc.

direct object (see object)

feminine (see gender)

gender

'Gender' indicates whether a word is masculine,
feminine or neuter. All nouns in German have gender.
   der Mann, die Frau, das Buch

imperative

The imperative is used to give commands or instructions
and also to make suggestions.
   Be quiet and **don't run!**
   Let's go to a nice concert.

indirect object (see object)

infinitive

The infinitive is the base form of a verb, which does not
show any person or tense. It is the form found in
dictionaries.
   (to) arrive, (to) buy, (to) have, (to) like

interrogative

Interrogative words are used to ask questions.
   Which train did you take? (adjective)
   Which do you prefer? (pronoun)
   Where did you buy it? (adverb)

intransitive (see transitive)

Konjunktiv

The German subjunctive has two types, **Konjunktiv I**
and **Konjunktiv II**. **Konjunktiv I** has present, future and
past forms and is used for indirect speech.
   *Sie sagte, sie **lese** die Zeitung.*

Konjunktiv II has a present and a past form and is used to express wishes, possibilities or doubts.

*Ich wünschte, er **wäre** hier.*
*Ich wünschte, er **wäre** hier **gewesen**.*

masculine (see gender)

modal particle

A modal particle is a word which indicates the speaker's attitude towards what is being said.

***Just** be quiet for one moment!*

German makes frequent use of modal particles, which include **doch**, **mal** and **ja**.

modal verb

A modal verb is used with another verb and expresses the speaker's attitude towards the action conveyed by that verb, such as ability or obligation to do something.

*I **can** do this on my own. We **ought** to leave now.*

negative

Negative words indicate that something is NOT done.

*I'm **not** staying. He **never** writes postcards.*
***Nobody** followed her. They said **nothing**.*

neuter (see gender)

noun

A noun is a word which names a person, a thing, a place or an abstract idea.

Peter, book, Hamburg, courage, love

number

'Number' indicates whether a noun, pronoun or verb is singular or plural.

***This is** my **book**. (singular)*
***These are** my **books**. (plural)*

object

The object of a verb is a noun or a pronoun which is affected by the action of the verb.

*I found **the keys**.* (direct object)
*I spoke **to him**.* (indirect object)
*I gave **him the keys**.* (indirect object + direct object)

participle

A participle is a form of the verb which can be used with other verbs, or as a noun or an adjective.

*I like **visiting** foreign countries.* (present participle)
*She has **finished** her work.* (past participle)
***Skiing** is exciting.* (present participle used as noun)
*He had a **broken** leg.* (past participle used as adjective)

particle (see modal particle)

passive (see voice)

person

'Person' is a way of classifying verb forms and pronouns.

***I live** in London.* (first person verb and pronoun)
***She lives** in New York.* (third person verb and pronoun)

Singular	*Plural*
I (first person)	*we* (first person)
you (second person)	*you* (second person)
he, she, it (third person)	*they* (third person)

plural (see number)

possessive

A possessive is a word which shows ownership or possession.

my, your, his, her, ... (possessive adjectives)
mine, yours, his, hers, ... (possessive pronouns)

prefix

Prefixes are syllables placed in front of a word which can add to or change its meaning.

*anti*body, *mis*understand, *un*fair

preposition

Prepositions are words such as *at, to, from, until,* which show the relationship between a noun or a pronoun and the rest of the sentence. Their position within the sentence occasionally varies in German.

gegenüber dem Bahnhof, dem Bahnhof gegenüber

pronoun

A pronoun is a word which is used instead of a noun, sometimes to avoid repeating that noun.

She lent me the car. I hurt myself.

My phone isn't working, can I use yours?

There are several categories of pronouns, including personal pronouns (*I, you, he, she, ...*), reflexive pronouns (*myself, yourself, ...*) and possessive pronouns (*mine, yours, ...*).

singular (see number)

subject

The subject of a sentence is the word or phrase which represents the person or thing carrying out the action of the verb.

Tom is learning German.

My best friend is coming tonight.

subjunctive (see Konjunktiv)

suffix

Suffixes are syllables added to the end of a word which change that word into a different part of speech.

tenderness; radicalize; beautiful

superlative (see adjective)

tense

This is the form of the verb which shows whether the action takes place in the present, past or future.

I live in London. (present tense verb)

I used to live in Berlin. (past tense verb)

I will move to Germany. (future tense verb)

Note that there is no simple relationship between tense and time; for example, the present tense can refer to present or future time.

transitive

A transitive verb (indicated by *v.t.* in most dictionaries) is one which takes a direct object:

*I **found** the keys.*

An intransitive verb (indicated by v.i. in most dictionaries) is one which does not take a direct object:

*We **danced** all night.*

Many verbs can be used both transitively and intransitively.

*We **ate** and then went out.*

*We **ate** a huge meal and then fell asleep.*

verb

A verb is a word which refers to an action or state. The form of the verb changes to show person and tense.

I cycle, she walks, we ate, they have finished

voice

The relationship between verb and subject is indicated by the use of either the active or the passive voice.

Many people witnessed the accident. (active voice)

The accident was witnessed by many people. (passive voice)

Although the meaning of both sentences is the same, in the active sentence *Many people* is the subject, while in the passive sentence *The accident* is the subject.

2 Spelling and punctuation

2.1 The German alphabet

■ **2.1.1** The German alphabet is read out as follows (pronounce the phonetic renderings as in German):

a	ah	**f**	eff	**k**	kah	**p**	peh	**u**	uh	**x**	iks
b	beh	**g**	geh	**l**	el	**q**	kuh	**v**	fau	**y**	üpsilon
c	tseh	**h**	ha	**m**	em	**r**	err	**w**	weh	**z**	tset
d	deh	**i**	ih	**n**	en	**s**	es				
e	eh	**j**	jot	**o**	oh	**t**	teh				

In addition the following four letters are used: the three Umlaut vowels ä, ö, ü and the letter ß (pronounced 'eszet').

■ **2.1.2** The Umlaut sign ¨ shows a change in pronunciation of the vowel. It occurs, for example, in the formation of many plurals, certain verb forms and some comparatives and superlatives:

das Buch	– die Bücher	*book, books*
lassen	– er läßt	*to let, he lets*
groß	– größer	*big, bigger*

■ **2.1.3** The ß is equivalent to ss. It exists only as a small letter (written SS when in capitals) and is used

- after a long vowel if followed by another vowel: fließen (*to flow*), gießen (*to pour*), Straße (*street*)

- after a diphthong if followed by another vowel: außen (*outside*), beißen (*to bite*), reißen (*to tear*)

- when immediately followed by a consonant: es gießt (*it's pouring*), ich mußte (*I had to*)

- at the end of a word: Fluß (*river*), er ließ ... zurück (*he left ... behind*), weiß (*white*)

Compound words are treated as if the individual parts of the word were independent:

Mißstimmung (*ill humour*), Kreissparkasse (*local savings bank*), Kreißsaal (*delivery room*)

2.2 Capitalization

The German use of capital letters differs in several ways from English usage.

■ 2.2.1 Nouns

In principle, all German nouns and words which are used as nouns begin with a capital letter:

der **M**ann (*the man*), die **D**eutschen (*the Germans*), der **A**lte (*the old man*), die **B**ekannte (*the acquaintance*), das **W**arten (*the waiting*)

Exceptions to the above rule include the following:

- nouns used as adverbs
  sonntags (*on Sundays*), **a**bends (*in the evening*), heute **a**bend (*this evening*), **a**nfangs (*initially*)

- nouns used in certain set expressions, including:
  alles **m**ögliche (*everything possible*), aufs **n**eue (*afresh*), bei **w**eitem (*by far*), im **a**llgemeinen (*in general*), in **b**ezug auf (*with reference to*), vor **k**urzem (*recently*), es tut mir **l**eid (*I'm sorry*), **s**chuld sein (*to be to blame*)

- adjectives used as nouns, where an accompanying noun is implied:

Nimmst du die braunen Schuhe?	*Are you taking the brown shoes?*
Nein, lieber die **s**chwarzen (Schuhe).	*No, I'd rather take the black ones.*

- the names of languages used in the following
expressions, where they are thought of as part of an
adverbial phrase and verb respectively:

  auf deutsch/englisch   *in German/English*

  französisch reden   *to talk French*

■ 2.2.2 Pronouns

- The polite pronoun **Sie** *(you)* (see 14.1) in all its forms
and the related possessive pronoun **Ihr** always begin
with a capital letter:

  Haben Sie Ihr Auto in der   *Have you been able to*

  Nähe parken können?   *park your car nearby?*

  However, note that the reflexive pronoun **sich** does not
  take a capital letter when it refers back to **Sie**:

  Wollen Sie sich nicht setzen? *Won't you take a seat?*

- The familiar pronouns **du** and **ihr** *(you*, singular and
plural) (see 14.1) in all their forms and the related
possessive pronouns **dein** and **euer** are written with an
initial capital letter in correspondence only:

  Liebe Susanne,   *Dear Susanne,*

    vielen Dank für Dein Foto,   *Many thanks for your*

    auf dem Du und Dein   *photo which shows you*

    Bruder mit Eurem   *and your brother with a*

    Kollegen zu sehen seid.   *colleague of yours.*

- The pronoun **ich**, unlike the English *I*, is not written
with a capital letter.

■ 2.2.3 Adjectives

In principle, adjectives begin with a small letter. This
includes adjectives of nationality, which in English begin
with a capital:

    deutsche Weine   *German wines*

Exceptions to the above rule include the following:

- adjectives forming part of a geographical name or the name of something unique
der **N**ahe Osten (*the Middle East*), der **S**chiefe Turm von Pisa (*the leaning tower of Pisa*), die **H**olsteinische Schweiz, die **D**eutsche Bundesbahn (*the German federal railway*), der **D**eutsch-Französische Freundschaftsvertrag (*the Franco-German Friendship Treaty*)

- adjectives formed from a place name by adding the (invariable) ending **-er**
der **K**ölner Dom (*Cologne Cathedral*), der **B**ielefelder Kinderchor (*the Bielefeld children's choir*)

- adjectives in titles
Königliche Hoheit (*Your Royal Highness*)

- adjectives in the names of special calendar days
der **H**eilige Abend (*Christmas Eve*)

- adjectives following **etwas, nichts, jemand, niemand**, etc.
nichts **N**eues (*nothing new*), jemand **F**remdes (*somebody foreign*)
except that **ander** does not take a capital letter:
etwas/nichts anderes (*something/nothing else*)

2.3 Punctuation

■ **2.3.1** The full stop

a A full stop is used in German

- after dates and ordinal numbers:
Montag, den **13.** August   *Monday, 13th August*
read: 'Montag, den dreizehnten August'
der **2.** Weltkrieg   *World War II*
read: 'der Zweite Weltkrieg'

- after abbreviations which are read out in full:

usw.	= und so weiter	*and so on*
z.B.	= zum Beispiel	*for example*
Dr.	= Doktor	*Doctor*

b No full stop is used

- after abbreviations which are pronounced as such:

  DM = (die) Deutsche Mark *German mark*
  read: 'deh mark'
  KG = Kommanditgesellschaft *limited partnership*
  read: 'kah geh'

- after weights and measures:

m	= Meter
kg	= Kilogramm

■ **2.3.2** The comma

In principle, the comma is used in German to separate all clauses within a sentence, whether they are main or subordinate clauses:

main	Wir redeten bis spät	*We talked late*
clause	in die Nacht,	*into the night*
subordinate	weil wir uns jahrelang	*since we hadn't seen*
clause	nicht gesehen hatten.	*each other for years.*

The most important exceptions to this rule are as follows:

a Clauses linked by **und** or **oder** generally do not have a comma between them when they are

- two main clauses sharing a common subject, which is not repeated:

  Ich kam Sonntag zurück   *I came back on Sunday and*
  und mußte gleich weiter   *had to go straight on to*
  nach Berlin.   *Berlin.*

- two subordinate clauses, whether or not they share a subject:

Sie gab ihm eine letzte Chance, obwohl er sie nicht verdiente **und** (obwohl er) sich nie ändern wird.	*She gave him one last chance, although he didn't deserve it and will never change.*
Er packte noch am gleichen Tag, da er die Miete nicht mehr bezahlen konnte **und** sein Wirt ihm keinen Aufschub gewährte.	*He packed his things the very same day, since he couldn't pay his rent any more and his landlord didn't grant him any further credit.*

b Infinitive phrases (see 31.1)

- An infinitive phrase consisting of **zu** + infinitive alone is usually not preceded by a comma:

Ich hatte keine Zeit **zu schreiben**.	*I didn't have time to write.*

However, if the infinitive phrase consists of more than just the infinitive + **zu**, a comma is required:

Die Dame bat mich, **ihr zu helfen**.	*The lady asked me to help her.*

- The verbs **brauchen** (*to need*), **haben** (*to have*), **pflegen** (*to be in the habit of*), **scheinen** (*to seem*), **sein** (*to be*) and **vermögen** (*to be able to*) are never separated by a comma from a following infinitive phrase:

Sie **brauchen** sich keine Sorgen um sie zu machen.	*You need not worry about her.*

Note that, unlike English usage, no comma is used after adverbs or adverbial and qualifying expressions such as **allerdings** (*however*), **erstaunlicherweise** (*surprisingly*), **im Gegensatz dazu** (*in contrast*), **meiner Meinung nach** (*in my opinion*):

Allerdings hat es mich doch sehr beeinflußt.	*However, it did influence me a lot.*
Im Gegensatz dazu schien Deutschland unter Adenauer stark und selbstsicher.	*Germany, in contrast, seemed strong and confident under Adenauer.*

■ 2.3.3 Other punctuation marks

* Direct speech is introduced by a colon. German speech marks are 'back to front' by comparison with English, and the opening set of speech marks is placed on the baseline:

  Dann sagte sie noch: „Ich bin gleich zurück." *Then she added, "I'll be right back."*

* An exclamation mark is traditionally required after an imperative (33):

  Nehmen Sie doch ein Taxi! *Do take a taxi!*

  Nowadays, however, a full stop tends to be used instead if the command is not a forceful one.

* An exclamation mark used to be traditional after the opening salutation of a letter:

  Sehr geehrte Damen und Herren!

  Liebe Sigrid!

  This is now usually replaced by a comma, in which case the first word of the following sentence begins with a small letter (see example in 2.2.2).

3 Numbers

3.1 Cardinal numbers 0–100

0	null	13	dreizehn	26	sechsundzwanzig
1	eins	14	vierzehn	27	siebenundzwanzig
2	zwei	15	fünfzehn	28	achtundzwanzig
3	drei	16	se**ch**zehn	29	neunundzwanzig
4	vier	17	sie**b**zehn	30	dreißig
5	fünf	18	achtzehn	31	**ein**unddreißig
6	sechs	19	neunzehn	40	vierzig
7	sieben	20	zwanzig	50	fünfzig
8	acht	21	**ein**undzwanzig	60	se**ch**zig
9	neun	22	zweiundzwanzig	70	sie**b**zig
10	zehn	23	dreiundzwanzig	80	achtzig
11	elf	24	vierundzwanzig	90	neunzig
12	zwölf	25	fünfundzwanzig	100	**ein**hundert
					or: hundert

- Numbers above 20 are written as one word, unlike English.

- **Null** translates as *zero*, *nought*, *nil*, as well as '0' in telephone numbers.

- The numbers 31–99 repeat the pattern of 21–29.

- Note the omission of **s** in the spelling of **sechzehn**, **sechzig** and of **-en** in **siebzehn**, **siebzig**.

- On the telephone **zwei** is often spoken as **zwo**, to avoid confusion with **drei**.

■ **3.1.1** The form **eins** is generally used in isolation:
Der Patient liegt auf Station *The patient is on ward*
eins. *one.*

It loses the **s** at the beginning of a compound number:

| Sie wird morgen **ein**undzwanzig. | *She'll be 21 tomorrow.* |

Cardinal numbers do not normally have endings.
However, the number **ein(s)** changes to agree with a noun.
It has the same forms as the indefinite article **ein** *(a, an)* –
see 5.1.3:

| Sie hat ein**en** Bruder und ein**e** Schwester. | *She has one brother and one sister.* |

Note that **ein** has no ending in **ein Uhr** *(one o'clock)*.

■ **3.1.2** In formal German **zwei** and **drei** have endings
when used in the genitive:

| Bei dem Zusammenstoß zwei**er**/drei**er** Autos wurde niemand verletzt. | *Nobody was hurt in the collision involving two/three cars.* |

In informal language and for larger numbers a dative
construction with **von** is used:

| Bei dem Zusammenstoß **von drei/vier** Autos wurde niemand verletzt. | *Nobody was hurt in the collision involving three/four cars.* |

■ **3.1.3** To indicate a particular year or decade, **-er** is
added to the cardinal numbers. Note that this ending does
not decline. It is often added to the figure rather than
being written out in full:

| In den 50er (fünfziger) Jahren begann das Wirtschaftswunder. | *The economic miracle began in the fifties.* |
| Die 68er-Bewegung begann als politisch motivierter Protest. | *The '68 movement began as a politically motivated protest.* |

3.2 Cardinal numbers 100 +

101 hundert(und)**eins**	2 000 zweitausend
121 hunderteinundzwanzig	100 000 hunderttausend
1 000 (ein)tausend	1 000 000 eine Million
1 001 tausend(und)**eins**	1 000 000 000 eine Milliarde

- **Eins** retains the **s** at the end of a compound number.

- Thousands and millions are separated by a space or a full stop, not by a comma as in English:
  3 789 560   10.594

3.3 Ordinal numbers

1. **erste**	11. elf**te**	20. zwanzig**ste**
2. zwei**te**	12. zwölf**te**	21. einundzwanzig**ste**
3. **dritte**	13. dreizehn**te**	30. dreißig**ste**
4. vier**te**	14. vierzehn**te**	40. vierzig**ste**
5. fünf**te**	15. fünfzehn**te**	50. fünfzig**ste**
6. sechs**te**	16. sechzehn**te**	60. sechzig**ste**
7. sie**bte**	17. siebzehn**te**	70. siebzig**ste**
8. ach**te**	18. achtzehn**te**	80. achtzig**ste**
9. neun**te**	19. neunzehn**te**	90. neunzig**ste**
10. zehn**te**		100. (ein)hundert**ste**

- The ordinal numbers (*first, second, third,* etc.) between 1st and 19th are formed by adding **-te** to the cardinals, those from 20th to 100th by adding **-ste**. The same pattern is repeated for numbers over 100.

- The forms **erste**, **dritte**, **siebte** and **achte** are irregular.

- The full stop after an ordinal number equates to *-st, -nd* or *-th:*
  1. = *1st*   2. = *2nd*   4. = *4th*

- Ordinal numbers are almost always preceded by the definite article and change to agree with a noun, like adjectives (9.2):

  Den zweiten Januar halte ich mir frei. *I'm keeping 2nd January free.*

3.4 Other numerical forms

- **erstens** *(first/firstly)*, **zweitens** *(secondly)*, **drittens** *(thirdly)* etc. are formed by adding **-ens** to the stem of the ordinal number (**erst-**, **zweit-**, **dritt-** etc.).

- **zu zweit**, **zu dritt**, **zu viert** *(in twos, threes, fours)* etc. simply use the stem of the ordinal number.

- **einmal** *(once)*, **zweimal** *(twice)*, **dreimal** *(three times)* etc. are formed by adding **-mal** to the cardinal number. Note that **eins** becomes **ein-**.

- **einfach** *(single)*, **zweifach** *(twofold)*, **dreifach** *(threefold)* etc. are similarly formed by adding **-fach** to the cardinal number.

3.5 Fractions

■ **3.5.1** Most fractions are formed by adding **-el** to the ordinal stem. They can be used as

- invariable adjectives (i.e. they add no endings):

  ein drittel Liter *a third of a litre*
  ein viertel Pfund *a quarter of a pound*

- neuter nouns:

  Ein Fünftel der Studenten fielen beim Examen durch. *A fifth of the students failed the exam.*

■ **3.5.2** The fraction **halb** *(half)* is declined like an adjective (9.2):

Ein halb**es** Pfund Steak, bitte.	*Half a pound of steak, please.*
Sie hat den halb**en** Tag geschlafen.	*She slept half the day.*

Compound forms such as **eineinhalb** and the more informal **anderthalb** *(one and a half)*, **zweieinhalb** etc. are not declined.

Es sind noch **eineinhalb/ anderthalb** Kiwis übrig.	*There are one and a half kiwi fruits left.*

Half can also be translated by the noun **die Hälfte**:

Die **Hälfte** des Essens blieb übrig.	*Half the food was left over.*

■ **3.5.3** With decimal fractions, a comma is used to indicate the decimal point:

23,55 DM	dreiundzwanzig Mark (und) fünfundfünfzig
24,5 km	vierundzwanzig Komma fünf Kilometer

4.1 Clock time in formal and informal contexts

In official contexts such as timetables, business meetings, opening hours, etc. the 24-hour clock is used, whereas in everyday speech most people use the 12-hour clock.

	formal	*informal*
14.30	vierzehn Uhr dreißig	halb **drei**
14.45	vierzehn Uhr fünfundvierzig	Viertel vor drei
15.15	fünfzehn Uhr fünfzehn	Viertel nach drei
15.50	fünfzehn Uhr fünfzig	zehn (Minuten) vor vier
16.10	sechzehn Uhr zehn	zehn (Minuten) nach vier
16.25	sechzehn Uhr fünfundzwanzig	fünf (Minuten) vor halb **fünf**
16.35	sechzehn Uhr fünfunddreißig	fünf (Minuten) nach halb **fünf**

Um wieviel Uhr geht Ihr Flug?	*What time is your flight?*
Um 13.20 Uhr.	*At 1.20 p.m.*
(spoken: Um dreizehn Uhr zwanzig.)	
Um wieviel Uhr kommst du?	*What time are you coming?*
Ungefähr **um** neun.	*At about nine o'clock.*
Unser Geschäft ist **von** 8.00 **bis** 18.30 Uhr geöffnet.	*Our store is open from 8 a.m. to 6.30 p.m.*
(spoken: ... von acht bis achtzehn Uhr dreißig ...)	
Wie spät ist es? Wieviel Uhr haben wir?	*What's the time?*
Es ist halb **eins**.	*It's half past twelve.*

4.2 Days of the week, months, seasons

Days of the week, months and seasons (with the exception of **das** Frühjahr – *spring*) are masculine.

■ 4.2.1 Days of the week

Montag	*Monday*	Freitag	*Friday*
Dienstag	*Tuesday*	Samstag	⎤
Mittwoch	*Wednesday*	Sonnabend	⎦ *Saturday*
Donnerstag	*Thursday*	Sonntag	*Sunday*

Samstag is nowadays more common than **Sonnabend** in North as well as South Germany.

For adverbs of time such as **heute** (*today*), **gestern** (*yesterday*), etc. see 11.2.2.

■ 4.2.2 Months

Januar	*January*	Juli	*July*
Februar	*February*	August	*August*
März	*March*	September	*September*
April	*April*	Oktober	*October*
Mai	*May*	November	*November*
Juni	*June*	Dezember	*December*

In order to avoid misunderstandings on the telephone, **Juni** and **Juli** are sometimes pronounced **Juno** and **Julei**.

■ 4.2.3 Seasons

The definite article is normally used with seasons:

der Frühling/**das** Frühjahr	*spring*
der Sommer	*summer*
der Herbst	*autumn*
der Winter	*winter*

4.3 Dates

■ **4.3.1** In correspondence, dates are normally written as figures using ordinal numbers (3.3). The following formats are used in business correspondence:

9. Juli 19..   (spoken: neunter Juli ...)
9.7.19..   (spoken: neunter siebter ...)

In private correspondence people generally give the name of the town, followed by the date in the accusative:

Köln, den 3. März 19.. (spoken: Köln, den dritten März ...)

■ **4.3.2** Note the use of cases and prepositions in the following phrases expressing dates.

- Spoken German

Der wievielte ist heute?	*What's the date today?*
Heute ist **der** dritte Oktober.	*Today is the third of October.*
Den wievielten haben wir heute?	*What's the date today?*
Wir haben heute **den** dritten Oktober.	*Today is the third of October.*

- Written German

Die Lieferung wird **am** 2. Juni ankommen. (read: zwei**ten**)	*The delivery will arrive on 2nd June.*
Die Tagung findet (**am**) Montag, **den** 17. Februar statt. (read: siebzehn**ten**)	*The conference takes place on Monday, 17th February.*
Sie wurde 1975 geboren.	*She was born in 1975.*
Wir haben **im Jahre** 1980 geheiratet.	*We married in 1980.*

Note that in German the year is never referred to by using the preposition **in** with the date alone.

4.4 Definite and indefinite time expressions

Expressions indicating a definite time point or period use either the accusative or a preposition + dative (15.2); indefinite time expressions generally use the genitive.

■ 4.4.1 Definite time expressions

jeden Tag/**jede** Woche	*every day/week*
alle zwei Stunden/Tage	*every two hours/days*
den ganzen Tag (lang)	*all day (long)*
diesen Freitag	*this Friday*
(**den/am**) nächsten Mittwoch	*next Wednesday*
am Morgen/Abend	*in the morning/evening*
am Tag/in **der** Nacht	*by day/by night*
im August/Sommer	*in August/summer*
einmal **am** Tag/**im** Jahr	*once a day/a year*
ab Dienstag/9 Uhr	*from Tuesday/9 o'clock*
bis Freitag/11 Uhr	*by Friday/11 o'clock*

Note that **an** (+ dative) is generally used with days or parts of the day and **in** (+ dative) with months and seasons.

■ 4.4.2 Indefinite time expressions

a Genitive nouns used as set expressions

eines Morgens/Abends	*one morning/evening*
ein**es** Nachts/eines Tages	*one night/one day*

Note: **eines Nachts** although **die Nacht** is feminine.

b Genitives of time treated as simple adverbs

morgens/abends	*in the mornings/evenings*
wochentags	*on weekdays*
montags, dienstags, etc.	*on Mondays, Tuesdays, etc.*
mittwochs nachmittags	*on Wednesday afternoons*

5 Articles

Like English, German has a definite and an indefinite article. The definite article is used to refer to a particular example of a noun:

der Mann *(the man)*, **die** Frau *(the woman)*

The indefinite article refers to an unspecified example:

ein Mann *(a man)*, **eine** Frau *(a woman)*

In German, both definite and indefinite articles agree with the noun to which they refer in gender (masculine, feminine or neuter), in number (singular or plural) and in case (nominative, accusative, dative or genitive – see 8 Nouns and cases).

5.1 Formation of articles

■ 5.1.1 The definite article

	singular			*plural*
	masculine	*feminine*	*neuter*	*all genders*
nom.	**der** Mann	**die** Frau	**das** Buch	**die** Bücher
acc.	**den** Mann	**die** Frau	**das** Buch	**die** Bücher
dat.	**dem** Mann	**der** Frau	**dem** Buch	**den** Büchern
gen.	**des** Mann(e)s	**der** Frau	**des** Buch(e)s	**der** Bücher

Common pronouns following the same pattern as the definite article (see 14.4.1 for forms) are:

aller *(all)*	jeder *(every)*
beide *(pl.)* *(both)*	jener *(that)*
dieser *(this)*	mancher *(many a)*
einiger *(some)*	sämtlicher *(all, entire)*
irgendwelcher *(some or other)*	solcher *(such, such a)*
	welcher *(which, some)*

For the declension of adjectives following the definite article (or pronouns which have the same pattern) see 9.2.1.

■ **5.1.2** Contractions of the definite article
Certain prepositions combine with the definite article in contracted forms if the article is not stressed, e.g. **am = an + dem**:

Ich warte **am** Kiosk auf dich. *I'll wait for you at the kiosk.*
An <u>dem</u> Kiosk habe ich eine *I waited for one hour at*
Stunde gewartet. <u>*that*</u> *kiosk.*

Contractions commonly used in spoken and written German are:

preposition	+ *dem*	+ *der*	+ *das*
an	am	–	ans
auf	auf'm*	–	aufs
bei	beim	–	–
durch	–	–	durchs
für	–	–	fürs
in	im	–	ins
über	überm*	–	übers
um	–	–	ums
unter	unterm*	–	unters
von	vom	–	–
zu	zum	zur	–

* colloquial use only

■ **5.1.3** The indefinite article

	singular masculine	feminine	neuter
nom.	**ein** Mann	**eine** Frau	**ein** Buch
acc.	**einen** Mann	**eine** Frau	**ein** Buch
dat.	**einem** Mann	**einer** Frau	**einem** Buch
gen.	**eines** Mann(e)s	**einer** Frau	**eines** Buch(e)s

The indefinite article has no plural form. The following have the same pattern as the indefinite article in the singular:

- **kein** (*no*), **irgendein** (*any*) when used with a noun

- all possessive adjectives: **mein** (*my*), **dein** (*your*), etc. (see 14.3.2)

For the declension of adjectives following the indefinite article (or words which have the same pattern) see 9.2.2.

5.2 Use of articles

In most contexts English and German use the definite and indefinite article in similar ways. This section highlights instances where usage differs.

■ 5.2.1 Use and omission of the definite article

a Abstract nouns
Nouns referring to an abstract idea as a general or familiar concept are generally used with the definite article, whereas it is normally omitted in English:

Die Kindheit vergeht so schnell.	*Childhood passes so quickly.*
Die Eifersucht machte ihm sehr zu schaffen.	*He suffered a lot from jealousy.*

However, abstract nouns are used without the article where

- the noun refers to the abstract idea in a specific context:

Das erfordert Kraft.	*That takes (some) strength.*
Unter Geschwistern gibt es immer Eifersucht.	*You'll always find (some) jealousy amongst brothers and sisters.*

- the noun is used in a proverbial sense (with some exceptions):

Sport ist gesund.   *Exercise is healthy.*
Übermut tut selten gut.   *Pride goes before a fall.*

but:
aus **der** Not eine Tugend   *make a virtue of necessity*
machen

b Geographical names
The definite article is used with the following:

- feminine and plural names of countries and regions, e.g.:
die Schweiz *(Switzerland)*, die Türkei *(Turkey)*, die Niederlande *(the Netherlands)*, die USA/die Vereinigten Staaten *(the United States)*, die Bretagne *(Brittany)*, die Lüneburger Heide *(Lüneburg Heath)*.

However, most countries are neuter and are used without the article, except when preceded by an adjective:
das neue Deutschland   *the new Germany*

- names of places or locations
Ich gehe in **die** Schule.   *I'm going to school.*
Die Bäckerei ist in **der** Stadt. *The baker's is in town.*

- names of streets, lakes and mountains
in **der** Forststraße; **der** Wörther See; **die** Zugspitze

c Time expressions
The definite article is generally used with time expressions, such as seasons, months and parts of the day (4.2):
Das Frühjahr beginnt am   *Spring starts on 21st March.*
21. März.
Der Juli war der heißeste   *July was the hottest month.*
Monat.

Den Nachmittag verbrachten wir im Botanischen Garten.	*We spent the afternoon in the botanical gardens.*

But when **Anfang**, **Mitte**, **Ende** are used with months the definite article is omitted:

Wir fahren **Anfang** August in Urlaub.	*We're going on holiday at the beginning of August.*

d Parts of the body and clothes

The definite article is frequently used with parts of the body and clothes, where English uses the possessive:

Er stand da mit **den** Händen in **der** Tasche.	*There he stood with his hands in his pockets.*
Sie zog sich **die** Handschuhe aus.	*She took off her gloves.*

e Names of meals

The definite article is used

- when referring to a particular meal:

Das Abendessen war ausgezeichnet.	*Dinner was excellent.*

  (The article is often omitted when referring to the meal in general:
  Frühstück gibt's von 7 bis 9. *Breakfast is from 7 to 9 a.m.*)

- with prepositions (see 5.1.2), except in some set phrases:

Zum Mittagessen haben wir Gäste eingeladen.	*We've invited guests for lunch.*

  but:

Übernachtung mit Frühstück	*bed and breakfast*

f People's names

The definite article may be used with people's names in informal speech:

Hast du **die** Petra gesehen? *Have you seen Petra?*

Der Herr Lehmann wohnt *Mr Lehmann doesn't live*
nicht mehr hier. *here any more.*

■ **5.2.2** Use and omission of the indefinite article

The indefinite article is used in English but is omitted in German

- with the verbs **sein** (*to be*), **werden** (*to become*) and
  bleiben (*to remain*) and a job title or nationality:

  Er ist/wird Ingenieur. *He is/will become an*
  engineer.

  Sind Sie Engländer? *Are you an Englishman?*

  Exception: where there is an adjective, e.g.:

  Sie ist eine gute Ärztin. *She is a good doctor.*

- after **als** (*as a*):

  Als Ausländer sieht man *As a foreigner you see things*
  das anders. *differently.*

  Als Mutter hat man es in *You won't find this job easy*
  diesem Beruf nicht leicht. *as a mother.*

- after prepositions used in certain senses, including
  gegen (*against*) referring to an illness and **ohne**
  (*without*). (English varies in its use of the article here.)

  Das ist ein Beruf **ohne** *That's a job without a future.*
  Zukunft.

  Gegen Depression läßt *There isn't much one can do*
  sich nicht viel tun. *about depression.*

- in certain set phrases:

  Das ist Geschmacksache. *That's a matter of taste.*

  Sie hat Kopfschmerzen. *She has a headache.*

6 Nouns and gender

A noun is a word which names a person, an animal, a place, a thing, an event or an abstract concept: **Tochter** (*daughter*), **Hund** (*dog*), **München** (*Munich*), **Schiff** (*ship*), **Geburt** (*birth*), **Mut** (*courage*). All nouns are written with an initial capital letter in German (2.2.1).

Nouns are classified as masculine, feminine or neuter. Since their gender is not always predictable, it has to be learnt for each noun. However, there are rules for determining the gender of some groups of nouns.

6.1 Masculine nouns

■ 6.1.1 Masculine by meaning

- male persons and male animals
  der Mann *(man),* der Bruder *(brother),* der Schreiner *(carpenter),* der Hund *(dog),* der Kater *(tom-cat)*

- names of days of the week, months, seasons, points of the compass and many nouns referring to weather
  der Montag *(Monday),* der Januar *(January),* der Winter *(winter),* der Süden *(south),* der Regen *(rain)*
  Exceptions: das Frühjahr *(spring),* die Jahreszeit *(season),* das Wetter *(weather),* das Gewitter *(thunderstorm),* das Eis *(ice)*

- makes of car
  der Audi, der BMW, der Rover

- alcoholic drinks
  der Brandy, der Cognac, der Schnaps, der Wein
  Exception: das Bier

■ **6.1.2** Masculine by form

Most nouns with the following endings are masculine:

-är, -and,	der Reaktion**är** *(reactionary)*, der
-ant, -ast	Doktor**and** *(Ph.D. student)*, der Fabrik**ant** *(manufacturer)*, der Pal**ast** *(palace)*

-el, -en (excluding nouns derived from infinitives and diminutives, which are neuter)

	der Mant**el** *(coat)*, der Mag**en** *(stomach)*
-ich, -ig,	der Tepp**ich** *(carpet)*, der Kön**ig** *(king)*,
-ismus, -ist,	der Kapital**ismus** *(capitalism)*, der Sozial**ist**
-ling	*(socialist)*, der Lehr**ling** *(apprentice)*
-or, -us	der Generat**or** *(generator)*, der Rhythm**us** *(rhythm)*

Common exception: das Labor

6.2 Feminine nouns

■ **6.2.1** Feminine by meaning

- female persons and female animals
  die Frau *(woman)*, die Schwester *(sister)*, die Katze *(cat)*
  Exceptions: das Mädchen *(girl)*, das Fräulein *(young woman, miss)* (these are diminutives; see 6.3.2)

- aircraft, airlines, motorcycles and most names of ships
  die Boeing, die Lufthansa, die BMW, die „Titanic"
  Exceptions: der Airbus, der Düsenjäger *(jet fighter)*, der Hubschrauber *(helicopter)*

- cardinal numbers
  die Sieben, die Achtundzwanzig, die Hundert, die Million

■ **6.2.2** Feminine by form

- all female job titles with the ending **-in**
  die Ärzt**in** *(doctor)*, die Physiker**in** *(physicist)*, die Köch**in** *(cook)*, die Sänger**in** *(singer)*

Note that an Umlaut (**ä, ö, ü**) is added to the masculine form where possible (**Arzt – Ärztin, Koch – Köchin**).

- most nouns with the following endings:

-ei, -enz	die Kart**ei** *(card file)*, die Intellig**enz** *(intelligence)*
-heit, -keit, -schaft	die Wahr**heit** *(truth)*, die Dankbar**keit** *(gratitude)*, die Leiden**schaft** *(passion)*
-ion, -tät, -ung	die Lekt**ion** *(lesson)*, die Universi**tät** *(university)*, die Warn**ung** *(warning)*

6.3 Neuter nouns

■ **6.3.1** Neuter by meaning

- young humans and young animals
das Baby *(baby)*, das Kind *(child)*, das Fohlen *(foal)*

- continents, countries, towns and regions
das heutige Europa *(contemporary Europe)*, das vereinigte Deutschland *(united Germany)*, das mittelalterliche Köln *(medieval Cologne)*, das historische Brandenburg *(historical Brandenburg)*
Common exceptions: die BRD *(Federal Republic of Germany)*, der Irak *(Iraq)*, der Iran *(Iran)*, der Libanon *(Lebanon)*, die Schweiz *(Switzerland)*, die UdSSR *(former Soviet Union)*

- metals and many chemicals
das Aluminium *(aluminium)*, das Eisen *(iron)*, das Gold *(gold)*, das Silber *(silver)*, das Chlor *(chloride)*
Common exceptions: der Stahl *(steel)*, der Schwefel *(sulphur)*, compounds with **-stoff**, e.g. der Kohlenstoff *(carbon)*

- letters of the alphabet and musical scales
  das A *(the letter A)*, das C-Dur *(C major)*

- fractions
  das Drittel *(third)*, das Viertel *(quarter)*
  Exception: die Hälfte *(half)*

- adjectives used as abstract nouns, and all infinitives
  and other parts of speech used as nouns
  das Skifahren *(skiing)*, das Gute und Böse *(good and evil)*,
  das beste Deutsch *(the best German)*, das Du und das Sie
  (the informal and formal you), das Auf und Ab *(the ups and
  downs)*

■ 6.3.2 Neuter by form

- all nouns with the diminutive endings **-chen**, **-lein** and **-el**
  das Mädchen *(girl)*, das Brüderchen *(little brother)*,
  das Zünglein *(little tongue)*, das Mädel/Madel *(girl)*

- most nouns with the following endings:

-icht, -ma, -ment	das Gesicht *(face)*, das Thema *(topic)*, das Argument *(argument)*
-tum, -um	das Datum *(date)*, das Stadium *(stage)*

  Common exceptions: die Firma *(company)*, der Reichtum
  (wealth), der Irrtum *(error)*, der Konsum *(consumption)*

- the majority of nouns (by no means all!) with the
  prefix **Ge-**:
  das Gebäude *(building)*, das Getreide *(grain)*,
  das Gespräch *(conversation)*
  Common exceptions: die Geschichte *(history, story)*,
  die Gewalt *(force)*

6.4 Compound nouns

Compound nouns are made up of two or more words. Their gender is determined by the gender of the last component word:

die Bahn + **der** Übergang → **der** Bahnübergang
(railway crossing)

die Bücher + **das** Regal → **das** Bücherregal *(bookshelf)*

6.5 Nouns with more than one gender

■ **6.5.1** Some common nouns vary in gender according to meaning:

der Band (*volume, book*)	das Band (*ribbon, tape, bond*)
	die Band (*pop group*)
der Erbe (*heir*)	das Erbe (*inheritance*)
der Gehalt (*content*)	das Gehalt (*salary*)
der Leiter (*leader*)	die Leiter (*ladder*)
der See (*lake*)	die See (*sea*)
die Steuer (*tax*)	das Steuer (*steering wheel*)
der Teil (*part of a whole*)	das Teil (*part of a machine*)
der Verdienst (*earnings*)	das Verdienst (*merit*)

■ **6.5.2** Some common nouns vary in gender without a change in meaning (due to regional variation or personal preference):

der/das Bonbon (*sweet*)	der/das Cola
der/das Gelee (*jelly*)	der/das Keks (*biscuit*)
der/das Joghurt (*yogurt*)	der/das Ketchup
der/das Liter (*litre*)	der/das Meter (*metre*)

7 Plural of nouns

In German, plural nouns are not distinguished by gender. The plural forms of German nouns are not always predictable and, as with gender, have to be learnt. The ways of forming the plural are:

Group 1: no ending, with or without Umlaut
Group 2: ending -e, with or without Umlaut
Group 3: ending -er, with or without Umlaut
Group 4: ending -(e)n (add -n if noun ends in -e, -el or -er)
Group 5: ending -s (often used for words borrowed from English or French)

There are some guidelines to which plural form is likely to apply. These are linked to the noun's gender and ending.

7.1 Masculine nouns

These have plural forms from groups 1–5 above.

■ 7.1.1 Group 1: no ending, with or without Umlaut

- The majority of masculine nouns ending in **-el**, **-en**, **-er** have no plural ending and no Umlaut, so their singular and plural forms are identical:
  der Löffel – die Löffel (*spoon*)
  der Wagen – die Wagen (*car, carriage*)
  der Fehler – die Fehler (*mistake*)
  Common exceptions: der Bauer – die Bauern (*farmer*) (see 8.2.3 a), der Muskel – die Muskeln (*muscle*), der Vetter – die Vettern (*cousin*)

- A few masculine nouns ending in **-el**, **-en**, **-er** have no ending but their stressed vowel takes an Umlaut, e.g.:
  der Apfel – die Äpfel (*apple*)
  der Bruder – die Brüder (*brother*)
  der Garten – die Gärten (*garden*)

■ **7.1.2 Group 2: ending -e, with or without Umlaut**
The great majority of masculine nouns belong to this
category, especially one-syllable words. About half of these
take an Umlaut. Examples:

der Arm – die Arme (*arm*)   der Fuß – die Füße (*foot*)
der Freund – die Freunde   der Vertrag – die Verträge
(*friend*)   (*contract*)

■ **7.1.3 Group 3: ending -er, with or without Umlaut**
This group is relatively small. These nouns form the plural
with an Umlaut where possible, e.g.:

der Gott – die Götter (*god*)
der Irrtum – die Irrtümer (*error*)
der Ski – die Skier (*ski*)
der Wald – die Wälder (*forest*)

■ **7.1.4 Group 4: ending -(e)n**
Most masculine nouns belonging to this group are 'weak';
see 8.2.3 for examples. Other common examples are:

der Schmerz – die Schmerzen (*pain*)
der See – die Seen (*lake*)
der Staat – die Staaten (*state*)

■ **7.1.5 Group 5: ending -s**
A few words have this ending, e.g.:

der Hit – die Hits
der Trend – die Trends

7.2 Feminine nouns

These have plural forms from groups 1, 2 and 4 above.

■ **7.2.1 Group 1: no ending, with or without Umlaut**
There are only two nouns in this group. Both take an Umlaut:

die Mutter – die Mütter (*mother*)
die Tochter – die Töchter (*daughter*)

■ **7.2.2 Group 2:** ending **-e**, with or without Umlaut

- Only feminine nouns ending in **-nis** or **-sal** add **-e** without an Umlaut. Words ending in **-nis** double the s in the plural.
  die Ersparnis – die Ersparnisse (*saving*)
  die Trübsal – die Trübsale (*affliction*)

- Some words of one syllable (and their compounds) take an Umlaut, e.g.:
  die Faust – die Fäuste (*fist*)   die Hand – die Hände (*hand*)
  die Frucht – die Früchte   die Wurst – die Würste
  (*fruit*)   (*sausage*)

■ **7.2.3 Group 4:** ending **-(e)n**
The great majority of feminine nouns belong to this category. Those ending in **-in** double the **n**. Examples:
  die Arbeit – die Arbeiten (*work*)
  die Freundin – die Freundinnen (*female friend*)
  die Reise – die Reisen (*journey*)

One noun also takes an Umlaut:
  die Werkstatt – die Werkstätten *(workshop)*

7.3 Neuter nouns

These have plural forms from groups 1–5.

■ **7.3.1 Group 1:** no ending, with or without Umlaut

- Nouns ending in **-chen** and **-lein** (diminutives), neuter nouns ending in **-el**, **-en**, most of those in **-er** and nouns of the form Ge-...-e take no plural ending and no Umlaut:
  das Schwesterchen – die Schwesterchen (*little sister*)
  das Kapitel – die Kapitel (*chapter*)
  das Essen – die Essen (*meal*)

das Muster – die Muster (*pattern*)
das Gebäude – die Gebäude (*building*)

- A few neuter nouns ending in **-er** take an Umlaut, e.g.:
  das Abwasser – die Abwässer (*sewage*)
  das Kloster – die Klöster (*monastery, nunnery*)

■ **7.3.2 Group 2**: ending -e, with or without Umlaut
This is by far the largest group. Apart from one exception,
das Floß – die Flöße (*raft*), these neuter nouns take no
Umlaut:

das Bein – die Beine (*leg*)   das Jahr – die Jahre (*year*)
das Ding – die Dinge (*thing*) das Spiel – die Spiele (*game*)

■ **7.3.3 Group 3**: ending -er, with or without Umlaut
A large number of neuter nouns belong to this group,
most of them one-syllable words. They take an Umlaut
where possible:

das Bild – die Bilder   das Gras – die Gräser (*grass*)
(*picture*)   das Haus – die Häuser (*house*)
das Blatt – die Blätter (*leaf*)

■ **7.3.4 Group 4**: ending -(e)n
Very few take this plural ending, the most common being:

das Auge – die Augen (*eye*) das Hemd – die Hemden (*shirt*)
das Bett – die Betten (*bed*) das Herz – die Herzen (*heart*)
das Ende – die Enden (*end*) das Ohr – die Ohren (*ear*)

■ **7.3.5 Group 5**: ending -s
A few words have this ending, e.g.:

das Detail – die Details
das Hotel – die Hotels

7.4 Double plurals

A few nouns have two plurals with different meanings, the most common being:

die Bank
- die Bänke (*benches*)
- die Banken (*banks*)

die Mutter
- die Mütter (*mothers*)
- die Muttern (*nuts for bolts*)

der Stock
- die Stöcke (*sticks*)
- die Stockwerke (*storeys*)

das Wort
- die Wörter (*single words of a language*)
- die Worte (*words in context/in a speech*)

7.5 Different uses in German and English

■ **7.5.1** Some nouns are singular in German, but their English equivalent is generally plural. Examples:

das Aussehen	*looks*	die Hose	*trousers*
das Benehmen	*manners*	der Lohn	*wages*
der Besitz	*possessions*	das Protokoll	*minutes*
die Brille	*glasses*	die Schere	*scissors*
der Dank	*thanks*	die Treppe	*stairs*
das Fernglas	*binoculars*	die Waage	*scales*

■ **7.5.2** A few nouns are used only or mainly in the plural in German. Common examples:

die Eltern	*parents*	die Lebensmittel	*food*
die Ferien	*holidays*	die Leute	*people*
die Flitterwochen	*honeymoon*	die Noten	*(sheet) music*
		die Trümmer	*rubble*
die Kosten	*cost(s)*	die Zinsen	*interest*

8 Nouns and cases

Nouns, as well as pronouns, adjectives and articles, are used in the four cases: nominative, accusative, dative and genitive. Cases are used in German to indicate the relationship of words to other parts of a clause or sentence.

8.1 Use of cases

■ 8.1.1 The nominative case is used

- for the subject of a clause or sentence:
  Der Apfel ist lecker.   *The apple is tasty.*

- for the complement of the verbs **sein** (*to be*), **werden** (*to become*), **bleiben** (*to stay*), **heißen** (*to be called*), **scheinen** (*to seem*) and the passive of **nennen** (*to be called*). For examples see 30.5.

■ 8.1.2 The accusative case is used

- for the direct object of a verb (the noun or pronoun that receives the action of a verb):
  Sie hat **einen Vorschlag**   *She made a suggestion.*
  gemacht.
  Wir haben **ihn** unterstützt.   *We supported him.*

- after certain prepositions (see 15.3, 15.4)

■ 8.1.3 The dative case is used

- for the indirect object of a verb:
  Ich gab **dem Kind**   *I gave the child the ball.*
  (*indirect object*) den Ball
  (*direct object*).

- for the object of certain verbs (see 30.3)

- after certain prepositions (see 15.2, 15.4)

■ **8.1.4** The genitive case expresses possession. It is used

• to indicate the owner of another noun, or to define or qualify another noun:

der Computer mein**es** Bruder**s**	*my brother's computer*
ein Haus mittler**er** Größe	*a medium-sized house*
die Auswirkung d**er** Magersucht	*the effect of anorexia*

• for the object of a small number of verbs (see 30.4)

• after certain prepositions (see 15.5)

• in some adverbial phrases (see 4.4.2, 11.1.4)

Especially in colloquial German, the genitive is often replaced by a construction with **von** (+ dative). With personal names both constructions are used:

der Hund von unserem Nachbarn	*our neighbour's dog*
der Deckel von der Kaffeemaschine	*the lid of the coffee machine*
Erikas Katze die Katze von Erika	⎱ *Erika's cat*

8.2 Cases of nouns: formation

Endings are added to German nouns to indicate some but not all of the cases in which they are used.

■ **8.2.1** The singular

Most nouns do not add any endings in the singular, except in the genitive singular of masculine and neuter nouns. This is formed by adding -s, or often -es with one-syllable nouns or for ease of pronunciation. (For exceptions see 8.2.3.) No ending is added to feminine nouns.

	masculine	neuter	feminine
nom.	der Lehrer	das Kind	die Hand
acc.	den Lehrer	das Kind	die Hand
dat.	dem Lehrer	dem Kind	der Hand
gen.	des Lehrers	des Kind(e)s	der Hand

■ 8.2.2 The plural

All nouns add -**n** in the dative plural unless their nominative plural ends in **n** or **s**:

    die Frauen – den Frauen   die Babys – den Babys

(The plural of most feminine nouns and all weak nouns (8.2.3) ends in **n**.)

		masculine	neuter	feminine
nom.	die	Lehrer	Kinder	Hände
acc.	die	Lehrer	Kinder	Hände
dat.	den	Lehrern	Kindern	Händen
gen.	der	Lehrer	Kinder	Hände

■ 8.2.3 Weak and irregular nouns

a Weak nouns

The so-called 'weak' nouns add the ending -**(e)n** in all cases, singular and plural, except the nominative singular. The (**e**) is omitted if the noun ends in -**e**, -**el** or -**er**. All these nouns are masculine. They include

- some names of human beings and animals, e.g.:
  der Mensch (*man*), der Bär (*bear*), der Bauer (*farmer*)

- many foreign words, especially those with the endings -**and**, -**ant**, -**at**, -**ent**, -**ist**, -**krat**, e.g.:
  der Automat (*machine*), der Demokrat (*democrat*), der Komponist (*composer*), der Student (*student*)

- many nouns ending in **-e** in the nominative singular, e.g.:

  der Bote (*messenger*), der Franzose (*Frenchman*)

	singular		plural	
nom.	der	Mensch	die	Menschen
acc.	den	Menschen	die	Menschen
dat.	dem	Menschen	den	Menschen
gen.	des	Menschen	der	Menschen

b Irregular nouns

- Eight weak nouns ending in **-e** add **-ns** in the genitive singular:

  der Buchstabe *(letter)*, der Friede *(peace)*, der Funke *(spark)*, der Gedanke *(thought)*, der Glaube *(belief)*, der Name *(name)*, der Same *(seed)*, der Wille *(will)*

- The weak noun **der Herr** adds **-n** in the singular (accusative, dative, genitive) but **-en** in the plural (all cases).

- The neuter noun **das Herz** adds **-ens** in the genitive singular, and **-en** in the dative singular and in all cases in the plural.

■ **8.2.4** Adjectival nouns

Nouns derived from adjectives retain their adjectival endings (see 9.2.1–3 for declension when preceded by a definite article, indefinite article or no article), e.g.:

der bekannt**e** Pianist	*the well-known pianist*
der Bekannt**e**	*the acquaintance*
ein bekannt**er** Schriftsteller	*a well-known author*
ein Bekannt**er** von mir	*an acquaintance of mine*
Ich habe das Buch **einem** Bekannt**en** geliehen.	*I lent the book to an acquaintance.*

9 Adjectives

Adjectives are words like **rot** (*red*), **weiß** (*white*) and **schmutzig** (*dirty*); they describe a noun. As in English, they can precede the noun or can be separated from it by a verb:

Ich ziehe die **weiße** Bluse an.	*I put on the white blouse.*
Die Bluse ist **schmutzig**.	*The blouse is dirty.*

9.1 Position of adjectives

In German, unlike in English, adjectives take different forms depending on whether they immediately precede or are separated from a noun in the sentence.

■ **9.1.1** When the adjective immediately precedes the noun, it adds an ending which changes to agree with the noun in number (singular or plural), gender (masculine, feminine or neuter) and case (nominative, accusative, etc.).

Das ist
- ein neu**er** Rock.
- eine schön**e** Bluse.
- ein schwarz**es** Kleid.

This is
- *a new skirt.*
- *a nice blouse.*
- *a black dress.*

■ **9.1.2** When the adjective is separated from the noun, it has no ending.

Der Rock ist **neu**.	*The skirt is new.*
Deine Bluse finde ich **schön**.	*I think your blouse is nice.*
Das Kleid ist **schwarz**.	*The dress is black.*

9.2 Agreement of adjectives

Adjective endings also vary according to the type of article which precedes them. The ending depends on whether the adjective is

- preceded by the definite article (**der, die, das**) or by words following the same pattern as the definite article, such as **dieser** (*this*) and **jener** (*that*) (5.1.1)

- preceded by the indefinite article (**ein, eine, ein**) or by words following the same pattern as the indefinite article, such as **mein** (*my*), **kein** (*no, not any*), **irgendein** (*any*) (5.1.3)

- not preceded by any of these.

■ 9.2.1 With definite article
Adjectives preceded by the definite article take the following endings:

singular

	masculine	feminine	neuter
nom.	der schwarze Rock	die weiße Bluse	das schöne Kleid
acc.	den schwarzen Rock	die weiße Bluse	das schöne Kleid
dat.	dem schwarzen Rock	der weißen Bluse	dem schönen Kleid
gen.	des schwarzen Rock(e)s	der weißen Bluse	des schönen Kleid(e)s

plural

nom.	die neuen Schuhe
acc.	die neuen Schuhe
dat.	den neuen Schuhen
gen.	der neuen Schuhe

- In the nominative and accusative singular the adjective takes the ending **-e** for all forms except the masculine accusative, which ends in **-en**:

Wo ist der schwarze Anzug?	*Where is the black suit?*
Ich finde den schwarzen Anzug nicht.	*I can't find the black suit.*

* In the dative and genitive singular and in all plural forms the ending is always -**en**:

Die weiße Bluse paßt zu dem roten Rock.	*The white blouse goes with the red skirt.*
Aber hast du den Preis der weißen Bluse gesehen?	*But have you seen the price of the white blouse?*
Hast du die schwarzen Schuhe gesehen?	*Have you seen the black shoes?*

■ **9.2.2** With indefinite article
Adjectives preceded by the indefinite article take the following endings:

singular

	masculine	feminine	neuter
nom.	ein schwarzer Rock	eine weiße Bluse	ein schönes Kleid
acc.	einen schwarzen Rock	eine weiße Bluse	ein schönes Kleid
dat.	einem schwarzen Rock	einer weißen Bluse	einem schönen Kleid
gen.	eines schwarzen Rock(e)s	einer weißen Bluse	eines schönen Kleid(e)s

plural

nom.	meine neuen Schuhe
acc.	meine neuen Schuhe
dat.	meinen neuen Schuhen
gen.	meiner neuen Schuhe

* In the nominative and accusative singular the adjective takes the endings of the DEFINITE article (**der, den**) in the masculine and has the -**e** and -**s** of the definite article in the feminine and neuter endings:

Das ist ein schöner Pullover.	*That's a nice sweater.*

Da hast du einen gut**en** Kauf gemacht.	*You've made a good purchase there.*
Ich habe ein neu**es** Hemd.	*I've got a new shirt.*
Hast du eine blau**e** Jacke?	*Have you got a blue jacket?*

- In the dative and genitive singular and in all forms of the plural the ending is always **-en**, i.e. the same as with the definite article. Remember that the indefinite article itself has no plural form. The plural endings are used with words following the same pattern as the indefinite article, such as **mein** and **kein**.

Das Hemd paßt nicht zu einer grau**en** Hose.	*This shirt doesn't go with grey trousers.*
Mir gefällt das Muster deines neu**en** Kleides.	*I like the pattern of your new dress.*
Das sind meine neu**en** Schuhe.	*Those are my new shoes.*

■ **9.2.3** Not preceded by any article

Adjectives not preceded by an article or related word take the following endings:

singular

	masculine	*feminine*	*neuter*
nom.	französisch**er** Rotwein	frisch**e** Milch	kalt**es** Bier
acc.	französisch**en** Rotwein	frisch**e** Milch	kalt**es** Bier
dat.	französisch**em** Rotwein	frisch**er** Milch	kalt**em** Bier
gen.	französisch**en** Rotweins	frisch**er** Milch	kalt**en** Bier(e)s

plural

nom.	neu**e** Schuhe
acc.	neu**e** Schuhe
dat.	neu**en** Schuhen
gen.	neu**er** Schuhe

Das ist französisch**er** Rotwein.	*This is French red wine.*
Hast du italienisch**en** Wein?	*Do you have Italian wine?*
Nein, aber ich habe deutsch**e** Weine.	*No, but I have German wines.*
Indisch**es** Essen ist oft scharf.	*Indian food is often spicy.*

These endings are the same as the definite article, except that the genitive singular masculine and neuter end in **-en**. However, these are rarely found outside poetic usage:

Froh**en** Mutes ging er an die Arbeit.	*He went off to work in good spirits.*
Schwer**en** Herzens verließ sie ihn.	*She left him with a heavy heart.*

■ **9.2.4** Spelling changes
Some adjectives have spelling changes when endings are added (see also 10.4):

- **hoch** loses its **c**: **hohe(r)**

- Adjectives ending in **-el** and **-er** lose their last **e**:

dunk**el**	dunk**le(r)**	*dark*
teu**er**	teu**re(r)**	*dear*

■ **9.2.5** Invariable adjectives
Adjectives formed from place names and numerals by adding **-er** are invariable (i.e. they add no endings):

Wir gehen zur **Leipziger** Messe.	*We're going to the Leipzig fair.*
In den **sechziger** Jahren gab es eine Studentenrevolte.	*There was a student revolt in the sixties.*

9.3 Adjectives and cases

Certain adjectives require the noun or pronoun to which they refer to be in a particular case. A fairly large group of adjectives take the dative case, a few take the genitive, and a very small group take the accusative. These adjectives almost always follow the noun or pronoun.

Meine Tochter ist **mir** (dat.) sehr **ähnlich**.	My daughter is very like me.
Er ist **des Mordes** (gen.) **schuldig**.	He is guilty of murder.
Werde ich **dich** (acc.) eigentlich nie **los**?	Shall I never get rid of you?

■ **9.3.1** Common adjectives taking the dative

ähnlich*	similar to	klar	obvious to
bekannt	familiar to	leicht	easy for
bewußt	known to	nah	close to
dankbar	grateful to	nötig	necessary to
fremd	strange to	nützlich	useful to
gemeinsam	common to	peinlich	embarrassing to
gleich	the same to	treu	faithful to

* **ähnlich** sometimes precedes the noun/pronoun.

■ **9.3.2** Common adjectives taking the genitive

bewußt	conscious of	sicher	sure of
fähig	capable of	wert	worthy of
schuldig	guilty of	würdig	worthy of

■ **9.3.3** Common adjectives taking the accusative

gewohnt	used to	satt	sick of
los	rid of	wert	worth

9.4 Adjectives with prepositions

A considerable number of adjectives are used with fixed prepositions. In the following frequently used combinations, the English preposition differs from the German:

abhängig von	*dependent on*
ärgerlich auf/über	*annoyed with*
begeistert von/über	*enthusiastic about*
charakteristisch für	*characteristic of*
gespannt auf	*curious about*
gewöhnt an	*used to*
höflich zu	*polite to(wards)*
interessiert an	*interested in*
schuld an (haben)	*(be) to blame for*
stolz auf	*proud of*
typisch für	*typical of*
verheiratet mit	*married to*
verliebt in	*in love with*
verwandt mit	*related to*

In constructions with adjectives the prepositions **auf** and **über** always take the accusative. (For the cases taken by prepositions see 15.2–5.)

10 Comparison of adjectives

Adjectives are often used to compare people or things. The three degrees of comparison are known as positive, comparative and superlative:

positive	comparative	superlative
schön (nice)	schöner (nicer)	der schönste (the nicest)
schnell (fast)	schneller (faster)	der schnellste (the fastest)

10.1 The positive

The positive form is used in comparisons of the type **so ... wie** (as ... as), **genauso/ebenso ... wie** (just as ... as) and **nicht so ... wie** (not as ... as):

Ein Bild ist **so** schön **wie** das andere.	One picture is as beautiful as the next.
Das Kleid ist **nicht so** eng **wie** das andere.	This dress is not as tight as the other one.

10.2 The comparative

The comparative is formed by adding **-er** to the positive form (e.g. **schnell + er**). The word **als** is usually used for than:

Dieser Anzug ist bequem**er** als der schwarze.	This suit is more comfortable than the black one.
Der Zug ist schnell**er** als das Auto.	The train is faster than the car.

Less than is expressed by the comparative form of **wenig** (**weniger**) plus the positive form of the adjective and **als**:

Sie ist **weniger** dogmatisch **als** er.	She is less dogmatic than he is.

The comparative is also used in the following expressions:

Du wirst **immer** größer.	You're getting taller and taller.

Je größ**er** du wirst,   *The taller you get, the more*
desto/umso schön**er**   *beautiful you are.*
bist du.

When the adjective immediately precedes a noun, the appropriate adjective ending (9.2) is added to the comparative:

Dieser Zug ist schneller.   *This train is faster.*
Ist das der schnellere Zug?   *Is that the faster train?*
Gibt es einen schnelleren   *Is there a faster train?*
Zug?

10.3 The superlative

The superlative is formed by adding **-st** plus the appropriate adjective ending (9.2) to the positive form:

Das ist die schnell**ste**   *That's the fastest connection.*
Verbindung.
Meinen schön**sten**   *I spent my best holiday in*
Urlaub habe ich im   *the Black Forest.*
Schwarzwald verbracht.

If the adjective is separated from the noun, **der**, **die**, **das** is generally used with superlatives plus the appropriate ending:

Klaus ist **der** schnell**ste**   *Klaus is the fastest.*
(Läufer *understood*).
Katarina ist **die** fleißig**ste**   *Katarina is the most hard-*
(Studentin *understood*).   *working.*

But where no following noun is understood, especially where something is being compared with itself, **am** is used and the ending **-en** is added:

Hier ist die Mosel **am**   *The Mosel is deepest here.*
tief**sten**.
Das Wetter war gestern   *We had the nicest weather*
am schön**sten**.   *yesterday.*

This form is the same as the superlative of adverbs (12.3).

10.4 Spelling changes

■ **10.4.1** Many common adjectives take an Umlaut (ä ö ü) in the comparative and superlative forms:

jung *(young)* jünger *(younger)* der jüngste *(the youngest)*
alt *(old)* älter *(older)* der älteste *(the oldest)*

The following common adjectives take an Umlaut:
alt, arg, arm, dumm, grob, groß, hart, hoch, gesund, jung, kalt, klug, kurz, lang, nah, scharf, schwach, schwarz, stark, warm

■ **10.4.2** In addition, the following adjectives have a consonant change in the comparative or superlative:

hoch *(high)* hö**h**er *(higher)* der hö**ch**ste *(the highest)*
nah *(near)* nä**h**er *(nearer)* der nä**ch**ste *(the nearest)*

■ **10.4.3** Most adjectives ending in **-d -t -s -ß -sch -x -z** add **-est** in the superlative for ease of pronunciation:

intelligent intelligenter der intelligent**este**
(intelligent) *(more intelligent)* *(the most intelligent)*
süß süßer der süß**este**
(sweet) *(sweeter)* *(the sweetest)*

but note:

groß *(large)* größer *(larger)* der größ**te** *(the largest)*

■ **10.4.4** Adjectives ending in **-el** and **-er** lose the last **e** before adding the comparative ending:

dunk**el** *(dark)* dunk**ler** *(darker)* der dunkelste *(the darkest)*
teu**er** *(dear)* teu**rer** *(dearer)* der teuerste *(the dearest)*

10.5 Irregular forms

As in English, there are a few completely irregular comparative and superlative forms:

gut *(good)* **besser** *(better)* der **beste** *(the best)*
viel *(much)* **mehr** *(more)* der **meiste** *(the most)*

Adverbs are used to modify the meaning of a verb, an adjective or another adverb. They can give information about time, frequency, place, manner and degree, reason and attitude.

11.1 Formation

■ 11.1.1 Adjectives as adverbs

In English, many adverbs are formed from adjectives by adding the ending *-ly*, but German uses the same form as the adjective:

Sie ist **schön**.	*She is beautiful.*
Sie singt **schön**.	*She sings beautifully.*
Ihre Stimme ist sehr **gut**.	*Her voice is very good.*
Die Tenöre passen **gut** zusammen.	*The tenors go well together.*

Unlike adjectives (9.2), adverbs add no endings.

■ 11.1.2 Formation from other parts of speech

Some adverbs are formed from adjectives, nouns, verbs and other parts of speech by adding endings. Common endings are **-erweise**, **-(s)weise**, **-lang**, **-lich**, e.g.:

glücklich**erweise** *fortunately*   stunden**lang** *for hours*
ausnahms**weise** *exceptionally*   erstaun**lich** *surprisingly*
teil**weise** *partly*

■ 11.1.3 'Original' adverbs

Many adverbs are not derived from other parts of speech:

time	manner/degree	place
heute *today*	äußerst *extremely*	dort *there*
jetzt *now*	besonders *especially*	draußen *outside*
zuerst *at first*	ziemlich *fairly*	unten *downstairs*

■ **11.1.4** Adverbial phrases

There are many adverbial phrases in German, mostly consisting of noun phrases (**den ganzen Tag** – *the whole day*) or prepositional phrases (**bei guter Laune** – *in a good mood*). Other common examples:

aus diesem Grund	*for this reason*
bei schlechtem Wetter	*in bad weather*
den ganzen Monat	*(for) the whole month*
eines Tages	*one day*
mitten in der Nacht	*in the middle of the night*
trotz des Regens	*in spite of the rain*
zu Fuß	*on foot*
zum erstenmal	*for the first time*

11.2 Use

■ **11.2.1** **Interrogative adverbs** are used to ask questions. They can be used to enquire about

a time, frequency or duration:

Wann fahren Sie in Urlaub?	*When do you go on holiday?*
Wie oft hast du gewonnen?	*How often did you win?*
Seit wann hat sie das gewußt?	*How long has she known this?*
Wie lange mußtet ihr warten?	*How long did you have to wait?*

b place and direction:

Wo hast du geparkt?	*Where did you park?*
Woher kommen Sie?	*Where do you come from?*
Wohin wollen Sie denn?	*Where do you want to go?*

Note that German differentiates between place (**wo**) and direction (**woher/wohin**), and also between motion towards (**-her**) and away from the speaker (**-hin**) (see also 11.2.4).

c manner and degree:

Wie habt ihr das geschafft?	*How did you manage that?*
Wie sehr ist er verletzt?	*How badly is he injured?*

d cause:

Warum/Weshalb ist sie nicht mitgekommen?	*Why didn't she come along?*
Wieso (*colloquial*) kommst du so spät?	*Why are you so late?*

■ **11.2.2 Adverbs of time** give information about when an event occurs. Here are some of the most commonly used, arranged in chronological order:

Damals fuhr ich einen Käfer.	*In those days I drove a VW Beetle.*
Ich arbeitete **früher** bei VW.	*I used to work at VW.*
Ich hatte **neulich** einen Unfall.	*I had an accident recently.*
Gestern kam der Brief von der Versicherung.	*The letter from the insurance arrived yesterday.*
Vorhin rief die Polizei an.	*A little while ago the police rang.*
Du warst **gerade** aus dem Haus gegangen.	*You had just left the house.*
Heute bin ich um acht Uhr aufgestanden.	*I got up at eight o'clock today.*
Gleich kommt Peter zum Frühstück.	*Peter is coming for breakfast in a minute.*
Später wollen wir in die Stadt.	*We want to go into town later.*
Für **morgen** haben wir noch nichts vor.	*We haven't yet made any plans for tomorrow.*
Bald macht das Geschäft zu.	*The shop will close soon.*

■ 11.2.3 Adverbs of frequency give information about how often an event occurs, on a scale from **immer** (*always*) to **nie** (*never*):

Sie ist **immer** freundlich.	*She is always friendly.*
Meistens ist er launisch.	*Most of the time he is moody.*
Wir gehen **oft** abends aus.	*We often go out in the evening.*
Ich komme **manchmal** zu spät.	*Sometimes I'm late.*
Ich spiele **ab und zu** Schach.	*Now and then I play chess.*
Einmal in der Woche gehe ich Schwimmen.	*I go swimming once a week.*
Bei uns schneit es **selten**.	*It rarely snows where we live.*
Ich bin noch **nie** Ski gelaufen.	*I have never skied.*

Other frequency adverbs:

täglich, dienstags, wöchentlich, monatlich, jährlich
daily, on Tuesdays, weekly, monthly, yearly
morgens, mittags, nachmittags, abends, nachts
in the mornings, at midday, in the afternoons, in the evenings, at night

■ 11.2.4 Adverbs of place give information about where something is located or takes place. They answer the questions *where?* and *where to/where from?*:

a Wo? *Where?*

Hier arbeitet Frau Nolte und **da** (**drüben**) Herr Meier.	*Mrs Nolte works here and Mr Meier over there.*
Unten wohnt der Vermieter und **oben** wohnen wir.	*The landlord lives downstairs and we live upstairs.*
Sollen wir **drinnen** oder **draußen** essen?	*Shall we eat inside or outside?*

Das Schlafzimmer liegt nach **vorne** raus und nicht nach **hinten**.	*The bedroom is at the front (of the house) and not at the back.*
Hast du **irgendwo** meine Schlüssel gesehen?	*Have you seen my keys anywhere?*
Ich habe **überall** gesucht.	*I've looked everywhere.*

Many of these can be combined to make pairs, such as:

hier vorn(e)	*over here*
da hinten	*over there*
hier unten	*down here*
da drinnen	*in there*

b **Wohin?** *Where to?*/**Woher?** *Where from?*

hin indicates movement away from the speaker, whereas **her** indicates movement towards the speaker:

Lauf schnell **hinunter**, Peter wartet auf dich.	*Quickly, run downstairs, Peter is waiting for you.*
Komm bitte **herauf/ herunter**!	*Please come up/down!*

These are normally shortened in spoken German to:

rauf	*short for*	herauf	*up*
runter		herunter	*down*
rüber		hinüber/herüber	*across*
raus		hinaus/heraus	*out*
rein		hinein/herein	*in*

Whether the movement is from or towards the speaker becomes clear only from the context.

Nach indicates movement towards a place, **von** movement away from it:

Komm, wir gehen **nach oben/unten**.	*Come along, we'll go upstairs/downstairs.*
Kommt dieser Lärm **von oben/unten**?	*Is this noise coming from above/below?*

■ 11.2.5 Adverbs of manner and degree describe how or to what extent an action is carried out. This rather broad category includes most adverbs with the same form as adjectives.

a   Adverbs of manner include:

Das hast du **gut** gemacht.	*You did that well.*
Kannst du **schnell** mal rüberkommen?	*Can you come over quickly, please?*
Sie hat **wunderschön** gesungen.	*She sang beautifully.*

b   Adverbs of degree include:

Er ist **äußerst** schlecht gelaunt.	*He is in an extremely bad mood.*
Das hat mich **besonders** gefreut.	*I was particularly pleased about that.*
Ihr Vortrag war **sehr** beeindruckend.	*Your presentation was very impressive.*
Das ist **verhältnismäßig** einfach.	*That's relatively easy.*
Ich fühle mich jetzt **viel** besser.	*I am feeling much better now.*
Das hat **ziemlich** lange gedauert.	*That took rather a long time.*

■ 11.2.6 Adverbs of attitude express a speaker's attitude to what is being said:

Angeblich hat er nur tagsüber Zeit.	*He claims that he only has time during the day.*
Glücklicherweise ist mein Auto nicht abgeschleppt worden.	*Luckily my car wasn't towed away.*
Leider kann ich morgen abend nicht.	*Unfortunately I can't make tomorrow evening.*

Ich komme **gern** ein andermal.	*I'd like to come another time.*

Many adverbs of attitude are formed from an adjective ı -**erweise** or end in -**lich**. Other common examples:

anscheinend	*apparently*
bedauerlicherweise	*regrettably*
dummerweise	*foolishly (enough)*
erstaunlicherweise	*astonishingly (enough)*
hoffentlich	*hopefully/it is hoped that*
komischerweise	*funnily (enough)*
meiner Meinung nach	*in my opinion*
meinetwegen	*as far as I'm concerned/for my sake*
möglicherweise	*possibly*
normalerweise	*normally*
sicher(lich)	*certainly*
vermutlich	*presumably*
wahrscheinlich	*probably*

There is also a large group of modal particles (see 16) which are frequently used in German to express the speaker's attitude but defy literal translation.

12 Comparison of adverbs

Only a few adverbs can have comparative and superlative forms. These include adverbs which take the same form as adjectives (see 11.1).

12.1 The positive

The positive form of adverbs is used in the same type of comparisons as that of adjectives (10.1), e.g.:

Das Stück gefiel mir **nicht**   *I didn't like the play as much*
so gut **wie** dir.   *as you did.*

12.2 The comparative

Regular adverbs form the comparative in the same way as adjectives, by adding **-er**, and they are used in the same ways (10.2), e.g.:

Sprechen Sie bitte laut**er**!   *Speak up, please!*
Er schreibt **weniger**   *He writes less neatly than I do.*
ordentlich **als** ich.
Je öfter du übst, **desto/**   *The more you practise,*
umso perfekter spielst du.   *the better you play.*

12.3 The superlative

The superlative takes the form **am** + adverb + **-st** + the ending **-en**. (Compare adjectives, 10.3.)

Er ist **am** schnell**sten**   *He ran the fastest.*
gelaufen.

12.4 Spelling changes and irregular forms

Like adjectives, some adverbs have spelling changes or irregularities in the comparative and superlative forms, e.g.:

oft	öfter	am öftesten	(see 10.4.1 & 10.4.3)
hoch	höher	am höchsten	(see 10.4.1 & 10.4.2)

As in English, there are a few completely irregular forms:

positive	comparative	superlative
bald *(soon)*	eher *(sooner)*	am ehesten *(soonest)*
gern *(gladly)*	lieber *(more gladly)*	am liebsten *(most gladly)*
gut *(well)*	besser *(better)*	am besten *(best)*
viel *(much)*	mehr *(more)*	am meisten *(most)*

Gern (+ verb) is the usual German equivalent of *to like* or *to be fond of (...ing)*. Its comparative and superlative forms **lieber** and **am liebsten** express preference:

Ich spiele **gern** Tennis, aber noch **lieber** spiele ich Squash.
I like playing tennis, but I prefer playing squash.

Am liebsten reite ich.
I like horse riding best of all.

13 Negatives

The most commonly used negatives are **nicht** and **kein** (13.1–3); for other negation words see 13.4.

13.1 Nicht

■ **13.1.1** **Nicht** is generally used to negate whole clauses. Its position in the clause is then as follows.

● It follows objects and adverbs:

| Ich verkaufe dir das Buch **nicht**. | *I won't sell you the book.* |
| Der Briefträger kommt heute **nicht**. | *The postman doesn't come today.* |

Exception: it precedes adverbs of manner:

| Das Stück gefiel mir **nicht** besonders. | *I didn't like this play very much.* |

● In clauses with a second verb element at the end, **nicht** precedes that element. This occurs, for example, with compound tenses, modal verbs and separable verbs:

Wir haben die Tür **nicht geöffnet**.	*We didn't open the door.*
Sie möchte ihn jetzt **nicht sehen**.	*She doesn't want to see him now.*
Ruf sie **nicht an**!	*Don't phone her.*

● **Nicht** precedes all other elements in the clause, including prepositional phrases and genitive objects:

| Geh **nicht in die Küche**! | *Don't go into the kitchen.* |
| Er wurde **nicht des Mordes** angeklagt. | *He was not accused of murder.* |

■ **13.1.2** Alternatively, **nicht** may be used to negate a particular element in the clause. It then precedes that element:

Sie kommen **nicht morgen früh**.	*They are not coming tomorrow morning (but another time).*
Wir stellen **nicht ihn** ein, sondern jemand anderen.	*We won't employ him but someone else.*

Nicht ... sondern (*not ... but*) is a common combination.

13.2 Kein

Kein (*not a, not any* or *no*) is the negative form of the indefinite article **ein**. It declines like **ein** and the possessive adjectives (see 5.1.3 and 14.3.2).

■ **13.2.1** **Kein** is the usual negation for nouns and is placed before the noun (and its adjective, if any):

Das ist **kein** guter Wein.	*That's not a good wine.*
Eva möchte **keine** Chips.	*Eva doesn't want any crisps.*

■ **13.2.2** **Kein** negates verb + noun combinations, such as:

Angst/Durst/Hunger haben	*to be afraid/thirsty/hungry*
Geld haben	*to have money*
Atem holen	*to take a breath*
Freude haben an	*to take pleasure in*
sich Mühe geben	*to make an effort*

Sie hat **keine** Angst.	*She's not afraid.*
Er hat **keinen** Hunger.	*He's not hungry.*

■ **13.2.3** It is also used in some idiomatic expressions:

Das Auto hat **keine 1000,– DM gekostet**.	*The car cost less than 1000 marks.*
Das ist **noch keine fünf Minuten her**.	*That was less than five minutes ago.*
Es ist **noch keine sechs Uhr**.	*It's not six o'clock yet.*
Er ist **kein Kind mehr**.	*He's no longer a child.*

13.3 Kein and nicht

In the following contexts either **kein** or **nicht** may be used. There is a slight difference of meaning, since **nicht** negates the clause as a whole, whereas **kein** negates the following noun and so puts more emphasis on it.

■ **13.3.1** With **sein** and **werden**

Er ist **kein/nicht** Direktor.	*He is not a director.*
Er wird **kein/nicht** Direktor.	*He won't be a director.*

However, the indefinite article **ein** is negated by **kein**:

Ist sie **eine** gute Sekretärin?	*Is she a good secretary?*
Nein, sie ist **keine** gute Sekretärin.	*No, she's not a good secretary.*

■ **13.3.2** With some expressions using **nehmen**

Platz nehmen	*to take a seat*
Rache nehmen	*to take revenge*
Rücksicht nehmen	*to show consideration*
Er möchte **keinen/nicht** Platz nehmen.	*He doesn't want to take a seat.*

■ **13.3.3** With prepositional phrases

Sie arbeitet in **keiner/ nicht** in **einer** Kneipe.	*She doesn't work in a pub.*

■ **13.3.4** With some common idiomatic expressions

Du sprichst **kein/nicht** Englisch?	*You don't speak English?*
Er spielt **kein/nicht** Squash.	*He doesn't play squash.*

However, **nicht** is preferred if the noun is seen as closely connected with the verb:

Sie fährt **nicht** Auto.   *She doesn't drive.*

13.4 Other common negation words

keiner	none	negates	einer
nichts	nothing		etwas, was
nie, niemals	never		einmal, mal
niemand	nobody		jemand
nirgends, nirgendwo	nowhere		irgendwo
weder ... noch	neither ...		sowohl ...
	nor		wie/als auch

The pronoun **keiner** is declined like **dieser** (14.4.1):

Wir konnten **keinem** von   *We couldn't help any of*
ihnen helfen.   *them.*

Keiner may also be used instead of **niemand**.

Niemand has the same optional case endings as **jemand** (14.7.7).

14 Pronouns

Pronouns are words used in place of nouns (see 6). They are usually divided into the following categories:

Personal pronouns **ich, du/Sie, er/sie/es** etc.
Reflexive pronouns **mich, mir, sich** etc.
Possessive pronouns **mein, dein, sein** etc.
Demonstrative pronouns **der, dieser, jener** etc.
Relative pronouns **der, welcher, was** etc.
Interrogative pronouns **wer?, was?, welcher?** etc.
Indefinite pronouns **man, jeder, mancher**

14.1 Personal pronouns

Personal pronouns refer to people or things and take the same gender (masculine, feminine or neuter), number (singular or plural) and case (nominative, accusative, dative or genitive) as the noun they stand for.

■ 14.1.1 Formation

	nominative		*accusative*		*dative*	
sing.	1. ich	*I*	mich	*me*	mir	*(to/for) me*
	2. du	*you*	dich	*you*	dir	*you*
	3. er	*he/it*	ihn	*him/it*	ihm	*him/it*
	sie	*she/it*	sie	*her/it*	ihr	*her/it*
	es	*it/he/she*	es	*it/him/her*	ihm	*it/him/her*
pl.	1. wir	*we*	uns	*us*	uns	*us*
	2. ihr	*you*	euch	*you*	euch	*you*
	3. sie	*they*	sie	*them*	ihnen	*them*

Polite form of *you (sing. & pl.):*

	Sie	*you*	Sie	*you*	Ihnen	*you*

Note that the polite *you* is always written with an initial capital.

The genitive forms of these pronouns sound archaic and are generally avoided in modern German; dative forms may be used instead. However, in historical and literary German the following genitive forms do occur:

sing.			*pl.*		
1.	meiner	*of me*	1.	unser	*of us*
2.	deiner	*of you*	2.	euer	*of you*
3.	seiner	*of him/it*	3.	ihrer	*of them*
	ihrer	*of her/it*		Ihrer	*of you* (polite)

■ **14.1.2** In most contexts German and English use personal pronouns in a similar way. However, there are some points to note:

a In German, the grammatical gender of a noun may not correspond with its natural gender. The pronoun always follows the grammatical gender:

Ich sehe **es** (das Kind) nicht mehr.	*I don't see **him/her** (the child) any more.*

b Indirect objects in German never require a preposition:

Kaufst du es **ihm** (dem Vater)?	*Are you buying it **for him**?*
Sie gab es **ihr**.	*She gave it **to her**.*

c People may be addressed either by the familiar **du** (sing.) and **ihr** (pl.) or by the polite and more distant **Sie**. There are no strict rules about when to use one or the other, but the following guidelines are usually observed:

* **du** and **ihr** are used when talking to children (up to about 14), friends and relatives.

* **Sie** is used in formal business contexts, when talking to acquaintances and strangers and by children talking to adults outside the family.

14.2 Reflexive pronouns

A reflexive pronoun reflects the action of a verb back to the subject or, rarely, to the object of a sentence:

Er hat **sich** einen Videorecorder gekauft.	*He bought himself a video recorder.*
Er hörte **die Leute sich** streiten.	*He heard the people arguing amongst themselves.*

Reflexive pronouns are used in the accusative and the dative. In both cases **sich** is the form for the third person singular and plural and for the polite form **Sie**. All the other forms are identical to the personal pronouns (14.1.1). For an overview of the forms, their combination with verbs, the case of the reflexive pronoun and its position in the sentence, see 27.

14.3 Possessive pronouns and adjectives

■ **14.3.1** A possessive pronoun replaces a noun and indicates its possessor:

Wessen Wagen ist das?	*Whose car is that?*
Das ist **meiner**.	*That's mine.*
Wessen Tasche ist das?	*Whose bag is that?*
Das ist **deine**.	*That's yours.*

The possessive pronouns (nominative masculine form) are:

sing.			pl.		
1.	meiner	*mine*	1.	uns(e)rer	*ours*
2.	deiner	*yours*	2.	eu(e)rer	*yours*
3.	seiner	*his/its*	3.	ihrer	*theirs*
	ihrer	*hers/its*		Ihrer	*yours* (polite)

For ease of pronunciation the bracketed **-e-** of **uns(e)rer** and **eu(e)rer** is usually omitted in speech.

Possessive pronouns take the same gender, number and case as the noun they replace. They are declined like **dieser** (14.4.1).

	masculine	feminine	neuter	plural
nom.	meiner	meine	mein(e)s	meine
acc.	meinen	meine	mein(e)s	meine
dat.	meinem	meiner	meinem	meinen
gen.	meines	meiner	meines	meiner

The alternative constructions **die meinige** and **die meine** belong mainly to literary usage. They are declined like the definite article plus adjective (9.2.1).

singular: der/die/das meinige/meine, deinige/deine, seinige/seine, ihrige/ihre

plural: der/die/das uns(e)rige/uns(e)re, eu(e)rige/eu(e)re, ihrige/ihre, Ihrige/Ihre

■ **14.3.2** Possessive adjectives (**mein, dein, sein** ..., *my, your, his/its* ...) are used with nouns (**mein Kaffee** – *my coffee*) and are declined in the singular like the indefinite article. The possessive adjective differs from the pronoun only in the masculine nominative singular and the neuter nominative and accusative singular.

	masculine	feminine	neuter	plural
nom.	**mein**	meine	**mein**	meine
acc.	meinen	meine	**mein**	meine
dat.	meinem	meiner	meinem	meinen
gen.	meines	meiner	meines	meiner

14.4 Demonstrative pronouns and adjectives

■ **14.4.1** A demonstrative pronoun singles out someone or something:

Welches Radio möchten Sie?	*Which radio would you like?*
Das/Dieses möchte ich.	*I would like that/this one.*

The most frequently used demonstrative pronouns are **dieser, diese, dieses** (*this*) and **der, die, das** (*that*). The endings of **dieser** are similar to those of the definite article (5.1.1). **Der** is declined like the definite article, but with slight differences in the dative plural and genitive:

	dieser (*this*)				**der** (*that*)			
	masc.	*fem.*	*neut.*	*plural*	*masc.*	*fem.*	*neut.*	*plural*
nom.	dieser	diese	dieses	diese	der	die	das	die
acc.	diesen	diese	dieses	diese	den	die	das	die
dat.	diesem	dieser	diesem	diesen	dem	der	dem	**denen**
gen.	dieses	dieser	dieses	dieser	**dessen**	**deren**	**dessen**	**deren**

Other demonstrative pronouns:

- **jener** (*that*): formal or literary, declined like **dieser**
  In dieser Stadt war **jener**   *That rogue was well known*
  Spitzbube·wohl bekannt.   *in this town.*

- **derjenige** (*that/the one*): formal, usually followed by a relative clause. Although written as one word, it behaves like definite article + adjective (9.2.1):
  Sie hat all **diejenigen**   *She visited all those who*
  besucht, die nicht   *weren't able to come.*
  kommen konnten.

- **derselbe** (*the same*): declined like **derjenige**
  Du machst genau   *You're making exactly the*
  denselben Fehler.   *same mistake.*

■ **14.4.2** Demonstrative adjectives, used with nouns, are declined like the pronouns, except that **der, die, das** (*that*) has exactly the same forms as the definite article (5.1.1):
  Hast du schon von **diesem**   *Have you tried this cake?*
  Kuchen probiert?

Der Vater **des** Jungen hat den Marathon gewonnen.	*The father of that boy there won the marathon.*

14.5 Relative pronouns

Relative pronouns introduce a type of subordinate clause called a relative clause.

■ **14.5.1** The most common relative pronoun is **der** (*who, which, that*); it is declined like the demonstrative pronoun **der** (14.4.1). Relative pronouns agree in gender and number with the noun they replace:

Der Mann, **der** eben hier war, ist mein Kollege.	*The man who was here just now is my colleague.*
Sind Sie **die Dame**, **die** vorhin angerufen hat?	*Are you the lady who phoned a while ago?*

However, their case corresponds to the function (e.g. subject or object) which they have in the relative clause:

Die Leute (*nom.*), mit **denen** (*dat.*) wir gesprochen haben, waren sehr interessiert.	*The people to whom we spoke were very interested.*

In German, unlike in English, the relative pronoun cannot be omitted:

Der PC, **den** wir gestern gesehen haben, war teuer.	*The PC we saw yesterday was expensive.*

■ **14.5.2** Other common relative pronouns
a **welcher, welche, welches** (*who, which, that*), used especially in formal writing as a variant of **der**, **die**, **das**, is declined like **dieser** (14.4.1) but not used in the genitive:

Der Minister, **welcher** die Sitzung eröffnete ...	*The minister who opened the session . . .*
Das Gebäude, **welches** ...	*The building which ...*

b **was** (*that, what*) only occurs in the neuter and is used

- usually after neuter indefinites such as **alles** (*everything*), **einiges** (*some*), **etwas** (*something*), **folgendes** (*the following*), **manches** (*some*), **nichts** (*nothing*), **vieles** (*a lot*), **weniges** (*little*):

Der Roboter macht **alles**, **was** man ihm sagt.	*The robot does everything (that) you tell it to do.*

- after neuter adjectival nouns and **das**:

Das Schönste, was ich je gesehen habe!	*The most beautiful thing (that) I've ever seen!*
Schreib genau **das, was** sie gesagt hat!	*Write exactly what she said!*

- to refer back not to a specific noun, but to a whole clause or narrative previously mentioned:

Sie ignorierte ihn, **was** ihn wütend machte.	*She ignored him, which made him furious.*

- to replace **das** in colloquial German:

Das Telefon, **was (das)** er sich gekauft hat, funktioniert nicht.	*The telephone he bought isn't working.*

- in the contracted form **wo-** + preposition (e.g. **womit**); see 15.6.3.

14.6 Interrogative pronouns

Interrogative pronouns introduce direct or indirect questions:

Wer ist das?	*Who's that?*
Sie hat nicht gesagt, **was** sie wollte.	*She didn't say what she wanted.*

■ **14.6.1** The most common interrogatives are **wer** (*who*), referring to persons, and **was** (*what*), referring to things.

Their forms are as follows:

nom.	wer	who	was	what
acc.	wen	who(m)	was	what
dat.	wem	who(m)	–	–
gen.	wessen	whose	wessen	whose

Was has no dative form and the genitive is usually avoided because it sounds archaic. For the contraction **wo-** + preposition used as an interrogative pronoun, see 15.6.3.

Although **wer** and **was** are singular in form, they can replace both singular and plural nouns:

Was suchst du?	*What are you looking for?*
Wer sind diese Leute?	*Who are these people?*

■ **14.6.2** **Welcher** (*which*) may be used as a pronoun or an adjective. It is declined like **dieser** (14.4.1):

Welche Bahn nimmst du?	*Which train do you take?*
Ich habe zwei Schläger.	*I have two racquets. Which*
Welchen möchten Sie?	*one would you like?*

■ **14.6.3** **Was für ein** (*what kind of*) can refer to things or people and may be used as a pronoun or an adjective:

Sie haben sich ein Auto gekauft. **Was für ein(e)s?**	*They've bought a car. What kind?*
Was für ein Mensch ist das nur?	*What kind of man must he be?*

Used with a noun, **ein** is declined like the indefinite article: **was für ein Mann/eine Frau/ein Kind** (5.1.3). As a pronoun **einer** is declined like **dieser**: **was für einer/eine/ein(e)s** (14.4.1).

The case of **ein** and **einer** is determined by their function (e.g. subject or object) in the sentence and not by the preposition **für**:

Was für **ein** Wagen *(subject,* *What kind of car is that?*
nominative) ist das?
Was für **einen** Wagen *What kind of car did you buy?*
(direct object) hast du
dir gekauft?

14.7 Indefinite pronouns

An indefinite pronoun indicates an unspecified quantity
or quality. For the negative indefinite pronouns **keiner**
(none), **nichts** *(nothing)* and **niemand** *(nobody)* see 13.4.

Common indefinites are:

aller, alle	*all (the)*	jeder(mann)	*everybody*
ander	*other*	jemand	*somebody*
beides, beide	*both*	man	*one*
dergleichen	*suchlike*	mancher	*some, many a*
einer	*(some)one*	mehrere *(pl.)*	*several*
ein bißchen	*a little*	sämtlicher, -e	*all (the)*
ein paar	*a few*	solcher, solche	*such*
ein wenig	*a little*	viel, viele	*much, many*
einiger, einige	*some*	wenig, wenige	*little, few*
etwas	*something*	welcher, welche	*some, any*
(coll: was)		wer	*somebody*
jeder, jeglicher	*each, every*		

Most of these function as pronouns but can also be used
with nouns. **Etwas, ein paar, ein bißchen, ein wenig** and
dergleichen and **desgleichen** do not change. The others
agree with the noun they refer to.

irgend *(some ... or other, any ... at all)* is used in
combination with many indefinite pronouns to stress
their indefinite meaning. It precedes **etwas, jemand** and
solcher as a separate word, but in all other combinations
it forms a compound word. The compounds decline in the
same way as the pronoun without **irgend**. Examples:

Hat er **irgend etwas** gesagt?	*Did he say anything at all?*
Hast du **irgend jemand/ irgendeinen** gesehen?	*Did you see anybody?*

The following indefinites frequently cause problems for English speakers.

■ **14.7.1 aller, alle** (*all the, everything, everybody*) is declined like **dieser** (14.4.1):

Alle sind hier.	*Everybody is here.*
Alle Arbeiter sind hier.	*All the workers are here.*
Sie war mit **allem** zufrieden.	*She was satisfied with everything.*

However, when **all** precedes **der, die, das** or another pronoun it usually does not change:

Ihr wißt nicht, was ihr mit **all dem/ihrem** Geld machen sollt.	*You don't know what to do with all that/all your money.*

■ **14.7.2 ander** (*other*) is mostly used as an adjective:
Das ist eine **andere** Sache.	*That's a different matter.*

The form **anders** is used after **sein** or as an adverb:

Diese Aufgabe ist **anders**.	*This task is different.*
Wir werden das Problem **anders** lösen.	*We'll solve the problem in a different way.*

■ **14.7.3 beide** (*both*) is usually declined like the plural of **dieser**:

Er hat **beide** (Autos) verkauft.	*He sold both (cars).*

After a definite article or another pronoun **beide** is declined like an adjective and often corresponds to English *two*:

Die/Diese **beiden** Männer haben uns geholfen.	*The/These two men helped us.*

The singular neuter forms **beides** and **beidem** also exist:
    Beides ist richtig.   *Both are correct.*

■ **14.7.4 einer** (*one, someone*) when used as a pronoun is declined like **dieser**:
    Eines der Kinder kam aus   *One of the children came*
    Spanien.   *from Spain.*

It is less frequently used as an adjective after a definite article or another pronoun:
    Mit **der einen** Hand hielt   *With the one hand he held*
    er sich an der Leiter fest.   *on to the ladder.*

■ **14.7.5 einiger, einige** (*some*) is declined like **dieser**, except that the rarely used genitive singular masculine and neuter are **einigen**. It is used as an adjective or a pronoun:
    Vor **einiger** Zeit war dort   *Some time ago there was a*
    ein Park.   *park there.*
    Er hat noch **einiges** zu   *He still has a few things to*
    erledigen.   *do.*

■ **14.7.6 jeder, jeglicher** (*each, every*)
These are used as pronouns and as adjectives. They are declined like **dieser**. **Jeder** is only used in the singular.
    Diese Messe findet **jedes**   *This trade fair takes place*
    Jahr im Januar statt.   *every year in January.*

■ **14.7.7 jemand** (*somebody*) takes the following forms:
    nom. jemand   *dat.* jemand(em)
    acc. jemand(en)   *gen.* jemand(e)s

The endings in brackets, and the genitive form as a whole, are used mainly in formal language.

■ **14.7.8 man** (*one, you*), is less formal than the English *one*:

| **Man** weiß nie, ob sie pünktlich kommt. | *You never know if she'll arrive on time.* |

Man exists only as a nominative; **einen** and **einem** are used for accusative and dative, and the genitive is avoided:

| Hier oben kann **einem** sehr kalt werden. | *You can get very cold up here.* |

■ **14.7.9 mancher** (*some, many a*) is declined like **dieser**:

| An **manchen** Tagen regnete es sehr. | *Some days it rained a lot.* |

If **manch** precedes **ein** or an adjective (especially in the singular) it usually remains unchanged:

| So **manch** ein Politiker wirtschaftet in die eigene Tasche. | *So many politicians line their own pockets.* |

■ **14.7.10 viel** (*much*), **viele** (*many*), **wenig** (*little*), **wenige** (*few*)

Viel and **wenig** are usually invariable in the singular but are declined in the plural like **dieser**. **Ein wenig** (*a little*) does not change.

| Für diese Arbeit bekommst du **viel/wenig** Geld. | *For this job you get a lot of/ little money.* |
| **Viele/Wenige** Leute gehen so früh zur Arbeit. | *Many/Few people go to work that early.* |

■ **14.7.11 welcher** (*some, any*) is declined like **dieser** and is used colloquially to refer to plural nouns or singular collective nouns:

| Hast du Streichhölzer/Brot? | *Have you any matches/bread?* |
| Ja, ich habe **welche/welches**. | *Yes, I've got some.* |

15 Prepositions

Prepositions indicate the relationship between one word (usually a noun or a pronoun) and the rest of the sentence. They determine the case of the noun/pronoun they are linked to.

15.1 Position

- Prepositions usually precede a noun or pronoun:
  Ich fahre **mit** dem Zug.   *I go by train.*
  Die Blumen sind **für** dich.   *The flowers are for you.*

- Some prepositions can either precede or follow the noun/pronoun: **gegenüber** (*opposite*), **entgegen** (*against, towards*), **entlang** (*along*), **betreffend** (*with regard to*), **gemäß** (*according to*), **zufolge** (*according to*).
  Ich wohne dem Rathaus   *I live opposite the town hall.*
  gegenüber.
  Die katholische Kirche ist   *The Catholic church is*
  gegenüber dem Rathaus.   *opposite the town hall.*

- A few prepositions always follow the noun/pronoun: **eingerechnet** (*including*), **hindurch** (*throughout*), **zuliebe** (*for the sake of*), **zuwider** (*contrary to*).
  Ich mache es dir **zuliebe**.   *I'll do it for your sake.*

Certain prepositions can also precede an infinitive phrase with **zu**: see 31.1.2.

15.2 Prepositions + dative

Nine common prepositions always take the dative:

aus *from, out of, made of*	nach *after, to, for*
außer *except, out of*	seit *since, for*
bei *near, with, at*	von *from, of*
gegenüber *opposite*	zu *to, at, for*
mit *with, by*	

Other prepositions which always take the dative are **abgesehen von** (*apart from*), **dank** (*thanks to*), **entgegen** (*against, towards*), **gemäß** (*according to*), **(mit)samt** (*together with*), **zufolge** (*according to*), **zuliebe** (*for the sake of*), **zuwider** (*against, contrary to*).

Common prepositions in context:

■ **15.2.1 aus** (*from, out of, made of*)

Sie kommt **aus** Berlin.	*She is from Berlin.*
Könntest du das Auto **aus** der Garage holen?	*Could you get the car out of the garage?*
Der Pullover ist **aus** reiner Baumwolle.	*The sweater is made of pure cotton.*

■ **15.2.2 außer** (*except, out of*)

Außer mir ist keiner im Haus.	*There is nobody in the building except me.*
Der Aufzug ist **außer Betrieb**.	*The lift is out of order.*

■ **15.2.3 bei** (*near, at, in view of*)

Das liegt **bei** Stuttgart.	*That's near Stuttgart.*
Er bleibt eine Woche **bei** seinen Eltern.	*He is staying for a week at his parents' house.*
Bei dieser Wirtschaftslage müssen wir Leute entlassen.	*In view of the economic situation we'll have to make people redundant.*

■ **15.2.4 gegenüber** (*opposite, compared with, towards*) usually follows a pronoun but may precede or follow a noun.

Ihm **gegenüber** lebte ein älterer Mann.	*Opposite him lived an elderly man.*
Die Bank ist **gegenüber** dem Supermarkt.	*The bank is opposite the supermarket.*

Gegenüber letztem Monat haben wir nicht schlecht abgeschnitten.	*Compared with last month we didn't do too badly.*
Ihr **gegenüber** ist der Vermieter oft sehr unhöflich.	*The landlord is often very rude towards her.*

■ **15.2.5 mit** (*with, by* (*using*), *at the age of*)

Ich fliege **mit** meinen Freunden in Urlaub.	*I'm going on holiday with my friends.*
Sie fährt **mit** dem Auto.	*She is going by car.*
In Deutschland kann man **mit** 18 den Führerschein machen.	*You can take your driving test at the age of 18 in Germany.*

■ **15.2.6 nach** (*after, to, according to, for*)

Nach dem Studium arbeite ich in Deutschland.	*I'm going to work in Germany after my finals.*
Sie fährt **nach** Hamburg.	*She is going to Hamburg.*
Nach Meinung der Experten ist das falsch.	*According to expert opinion, this is wrong.*

Note that in the set phrase **meiner Meinung nach** (*in my opinion*) the preposition follows the noun.

Er strebt **nach** sozialem Prestige.	*He strives for social prestige.*

■ **15.2.7 seit** (*since, for*)

Ich warte **seit** Montag auf die Lieferung.	*I have been waiting for the delivery since Monday.*
Er ist **seit** zwei Tagen krank.	*He has been ill for two days.*

Note that in German the present tense is used for past actions continuing up to the present (18.1.1).

■ **15.2.8 von** (*from, of, about, by* in passive constructions)

Ich habe einen Brief **von** der Bank bekommen.	*I've received a letter from the bank.*
Einige **von** deinen Kollegen sind nicht sehr freundlich.	*Some of your colleagues are not very friendly.*

As here, **von** is often used (especially in colloquial German) instead of the genitive case (**einige deiner Kollegen**).

Sie sprechen **von** dem Geld, das sie verdient haben.	*They are talking about the money they earned.*
Das Fax wurde **von** mir persönlich abgeschickt.	*The fax was sent by me personally.*

■ **15.2.9 zu** (*to, at, for*)

Sie ist **zu** ihrem Freund gegangen.	*She has gone to her boyfriend.*
Zu diesem Preis kaufe ich das nicht.	*I'm not buying it at this price.*
Was hat er **zum** Geburtstag bekommen?	*What did he get for his birthday?*

15.3 Prepositions + accusative

Six common prepositions always take the accusative:

bis *until, as far as, by*	gegen *against, towards*
durch *through, by*	ohne *without*
für *for*	um *(a)round, at*

Other prepositions always taking the accusative are **betreffend** (*with regard to*), **eingerechnet** (*including*), **hindurch** (*throughout*), **wider** (*against, contrary to*).

Common prepositions in context:

■ **15.3.1 bis** (*until, as far as, by*)

Deutschland war **bis** 1990 geteilt.	*Germany was divided until 1990.*

| Diese Maschine fliegt nur **bis** New York. | *This aircraft is only going as far as New York.* |
| **Bis** 19 Uhr muß das Abendessen fertig sein. | *Dinner will have to be ready by seven o'clock.* |

Note that **bis** can only be used on its own in a few specific contexts. Otherwise, **bis auf** or **bis zu** are commonly used.

■ **15.3.2 durch** (*through, by* in passive constructions)

| Die Reise **durch** den Tunnel ist kürzer. | *The journey through the tunnel is shorter.* |
| Wurdest du **durch** den Lärm gestört? | *Were you disturbed by the noise?* |

■ **15.3.3 für** (*for*)

| Diese CD habe ich **für** meinen Freund gekauft. | *I bought this CD for my friend.* |

■ **15.3.4 gegen** (*against, contrary to, about, compared to, in exchange for, towards*)

Wir demonstrieren **gegen** den Rassismus.	*We are demonstrating against racism.*
Gegen alle Erwartungen wurde Rover von BMW übernommen.	*Contrary to all expectations, Rover was taken over by BMW.*
Ich werde **gegen** 5 Uhr da sein.	*I'll be there at about 5.*
Gegen dich ist er ein Versager.	*Compared to you he is a loser.*
Sie können das **gegen** einen Gutschein eintauschen.	*You can exchange that for a credit note.*
Wir planen ein Treffen **gegen** Ende Januar.	*We are planning to meet towards the end of January.*

■ **15.3.5 ohne** (*without*)

Er ist **ohne** seine Frau nach Hamburg gefahren.	*He went to Hamburg without his wife.*

■ **15.3.6 um** (*round, around, at* preceding clock times, *by*)

Das Kino ist **um** die Ecke.	*The cinema is round the corner.*
Amerigo Vespucci hat Amerika **um** 1500 erreicht.	*Amerigo Vespucci reached America around 1500.*
Um 9.00 Uhr muß ich zur Arbeit.	*I'll have to go to work at nine o'clock.*
Der Termin kann nicht **um** drei Wochen verschoben werden.	*The deadline cannot be postponed by three weeks.*

15.4 Prepositions + dative or accusative

The most common prepositions in this group are:

an *on, at*	in *in*	unter *under, below*
auf *on*	neben *beside*	vor *in front of*
hinter *behind*	über *over, above*	zwischen *between*

These nine prepositions usually take the dative when indicating position in a particular place and the accusative when expressing a change of position:

Das Buch liegt **auf dem** Tisch (dat.).	*The book is on the table.*
Ich lege das Buch **auf den** Tisch (acc.).	*I'll put the book on the table.*

If there is no reference to place, **auf** and **über** are used with the accusative, the others generally with the dative.

Other prepositions taking either the dative or the accusative are **ab** (*from*): takes the dative for indications of place, otherwise (rarely) the accusative; and **entlang** (*along*): takes the dative when it precedes the noun, but it usually follows the noun and takes the accusative.

Common prepositions in context:

■ 15.4.1 an

- *on (+ acc. or dat.)*

Das Bild hängt schon **an** der Wand *(dat.)*.	*The picture is already hanging on the wall.*
Er hat es gestern **an** die Wand gehängt *(acc.)*.	*He hung it on the wall yesterday.*
Ich komme **am** Mittwoch *(dat.)*.	*I'll come on Wednesday.*

- *at (+ dat.)*

Sie hat **an** der Universität Trier studiert.	*She studied at Trier University.*

- *to (+ acc.)*

Haben Sie die Waren **an** die Sekretärin geschickt?	*Did you send the goods to the secretary?*

■ 15.4.2 auf

- *on (+ acc. or dat.)*

Bist du **auf** den Boden *(acc.)* gefallen?	*Did you fall on the floor?*
Warum sitzt du **auf** dem Boden *(dat.)*?	*Why are you sitting on the floor?*

- *at, for, in, to (+ acc.)*

Auf seine Bitte gingen wir alle zur Kirche.	*At his request we all went to church.*
Auf das Geld wirst du lange warten müssen.	*You will have to wait a long time for the money.*
Was heißt 'ivy' **auf** deutsch?	*What is the word for 'ivy' in German?*
Wie reagieren wir **auf** diese Mahnung?	*How do we react to this reminder?*

■ **15.4.3 hinter** (*behind*)

Hinter dem Wald *(dat.)* *There is a very fine lake*
liegt ein sehr schöner See. *beyond the forest.*
Ich stelle die Schubkarre *I'll put the wheelbarrow*
hinter den Schuppen *(acc.)*. *behind the shed.*

■ **15.4.4 in** (*in, into, to*)

Petra spielt **in** dem *Petra is playing in the garden.*
Garten *(dat.)*.
Sie läuft **in** den Garten *She is running into the garden.*
(acc.).
Wir gehen **ins** Restaurant *We are going to the restaurant.*
(acc.).

■ **15.4.5 neben** (*beside, next to*)

Die Fernbedienung liegt *The remote control is*
neben dem Sessel *(dat.)*. *beside the armchair.*
Er setzte sich **neben** den *He sat down next to the*
Geschäftsführer *(acc.)*. *managing director.*

If there is movement but no change of place in relation to
the noun following the preposition, the dative is used:

Er ging **neben** ihr *(dat.)* her. *He walked beside her.*

■ **15.4.6 über**

• *over, above (+ acc. or dat.)*
Über der Synagoge *(dat.)* *Above the synagogue*
war ein Judenstern. *there was a star of David.*
Dieses Flugzeug fliegt in *This plane flies over the*
nur sechs Stunden **über** *Atlantic in only six hours.*
den Atlantik *(acc.)*.
Der Hubschrauber kreiste *The helicopter circled*
eine Stunde **über** der *above the city for one hour.*
Stadt *(dat.)*.

- *about, via (+ acc.)*
  Laß uns **über** etwas
  anderes sprechen.
  Wir fahren **über** Hannover.

  *Let's talk about something
  different.*
  We are going via Hanover.

■ 15.4.7 unter

- *under, below (+ acc. or dat.)*
  Ich fand es **unter** dem
  Tisch *(dat.)*.
  Die Katze ist **unter** den
  Tisch *(acc.)* gelaufen.

  I found it under the table.

  The cat ran under the table.

- *among, given (+ dat.)*
  Unter diesen Leuten ist
  keiner, den ich kenne.
  Unter diesen Umständen
  können wir das Projekt
  nicht zu Ende führen.

  *There is no one I know among
  these people.*
  *Given such circumstances we
  cannot complete the project.*

■ 15.4.8 vor

- *in front of (+ acc. or dat.)*
  Viele Kunden warteten **vor**
  der Kasse *(dat.)*.

  *Many customers were
  waiting in front of the
  checkout.*

- *before, of (+ dat.)*
  Ich möchte **vor** der
  Stunde mit dir sprechen.
  Sie hat Angst **vor** dem
  Fliegen.

  *I would like to talk to you
  before the class.*
  She is afraid of flying.

■ **15.4.9 zwischen** (*between*)

Der Brief liegt **zwischen** den Akten (*dat.*)	*The letter is between the files.*
Ich habe die Lampe **zwischen** die Sessel (*acc.*) gestellt.	*I've placed the lamp between the armchairs.*

15.5 Prepositions + genitive

Four common prepositions take the genitive:

(an)statt *instead of*	während *during*
trotz *in spite of*	wegen *because of*

All four may also be used with the dative in colloquial German:

Während des Essens/dem Essen (*gen./dat.*) wird nicht gespielt.	*You don't play during mealtimes.*

Other prepositions taking the genitive are **anstelle** (*instead of*), **aufgrund** (*because of*), **außerhalb** (*outside*), **beiderseits** (*on both sides of*), **diesseits** (*on this side of*), **halber** (*for the sake of, because of* – follows the noun), **infolge** (*in consequence of*), **innerhalb** (*inside, within*), **jenseits** (*on the other side of*), **mangels** (*for want of*), **oberhalb** (*above*), **unterhalb** (*below*), **um … willen** (*for the sake of*), **zugunsten** (*for the benefit of*), **zwecks** (*for the purpose of*).

Common prepositions in context:

■ **15.5.1 (an)statt** (*instead of*)

Statt des Managers ist ein Verkäufer gekommen.	*A shop assistant came instead of the manager.*

■ **15.5.2** trotz (*in spite of*)

Trotz all seiner
Bemühungen konnte die
Arbeit nicht rechtzeitig
fertiggestellt werden.

*In spite of all his efforts the work
could not be finished on time.*

■ **15.5.3** während (*during*)

Sie war sehr nervös
während des
Vorstellungsgesprächs.

*She was very nervous during
the interview.*

■ **15.5.4** wegen (*because of, about, concerning*)

Wir sind **wegen** des
Regens nicht in die Stadt
gegangen.

*We didn't go into town because
of the rain.*

Wir müssen noch **wegen**
des Termins miteinander
sprechen.

*We still have to talk about the
date.*

15.6 Contracted and combined forms

Prepositions are invariable in form. However, they can combine with other words in the following ways.

■ **15.6.1** Some common prepositions often form contractions with the definite article (e.g. **zu** + **dem** = **zum**): see 5.1.2.

■ **15.6.2** In place of the following prepositions plus the pronouns 'it' or 'them' (referring to things, not people), a single word is formed from **da-** + the preposition: **dabei**, **dadurch**, **dafür**, **dagegen**, **dahinter**, **damit**, **danach**, **daneben**, **davon**, **davor**, **dazu**, **dazwischen**.

An **r** is inserted if the preposition begins with a vowel:
daran, darauf, daraus, darin, darum, darunter, darüber.

Bist du **damit** einverstanden?	*Do you agree with it?*
Das sind meine Vorschläge, können wir **darüber** sprechen?	*These are my suggestions; can we talk about them?*

The **da-** forms are also used

* to refer to a specific group of people:

Ich erwarte acht Gäste, **darunter** zwei Schauspieler.	*I am expecting eight guests, among them two actors.*

* to refer back to a preceding sentence/clause:

Seid ihr **damit** einverstanden?	*Do you agree with that?*

* to refer forward to a following clause:

Ich freue mich **darauf**, daß ...	*I'm looking forward to ...*

■ **15.6.3** In place of a preposition plus the question word
was? *(what?)* a single word is formed from **wo(r)-** +
preposition with the same prepositions as above (15.6.2).

Wozu brauchst du das?	*What do you need this for?*
Worüber haben sie gesprochen?	*What did they talk about?*

This form is also used for a preposition plus the relative
pronoun **was** *(which, that)*, referring to things, not people:

Das Buch, **worüber** wir gesprochen haben, ist hier.	*The book (that) we talked about is here.*

16 Modal particles

Modal particles are words which express the speaker's attitude to what he or she is saying. They may, for example, convey agreement or disagreement, express surprise, or emphasize or tone down a statement. They are used extensively in German.

There are no standard translations for these particles. English tends to use intonation, stress, tag-questions (e.g. *isn't it?*) and phrases such as *you know* and *you see* as equivalents. The most common modal particles are listed below, with examples.

16.1 aber

■ **16.1.1** In exclamations **aber** indicates that something unexpected has happened:

Das ist **aber** schade!	*Oh, what a shame!*
Bist du **aber** gewachsen!	*Haven't you grown!*

■ **16.1.2** In statements and commands **aber** has the same meaning as the conjunction **aber** (*but*), expressing a contradiction or a reminder, but it is placed within the clause:

Du mußt **aber** zur Polizei gehen.	*You must go to the police, though.*
Paß **aber** auf dein Geld auf!	*But do watch your money!*

16.2 auch

■ **16.2.1** In statements **auch** may confirm, correct or contradict a preceding phrase or sentence:

Er hat **auch** sehr viel geraucht.	*He did smoke an awful lot.*
Das hat sie **auch** nicht gemeint.	*But that's not what she meant.*

■ **16.2.2** In 'yes/no' questions **auch** seeks confirmation that something is/is not the case:

Haben Sie **auch** den Schlüssel abgegeben?	*You did hand in the key, didn't you?*
Hast du dich **auch** nicht geirrt?	*Are you sure you haven't made a mistake?*

■ **16.2.3** In questions with an interrogative word **auch** expresses a negative attitude:

Warum mußte sie **auch** Lehrerin werden?	*Why on earth did she have to become a teacher?*
Was kannst du **auch** von so jemandem erwarten?	*Well, what do you expect from someone like that?*

16.3 bloß and nur

Bloß and **nur** are in most cases interchangeable.

■ **16.3.1** In imperatives **bloß** and **nur** often express warning and disapproval, but can also convey reassurance:

Versuch das **bloß/nur** noch mal!	*Just you try that again!*
Mach dir **bloß/nur** keine Sorgen!	*Just don't worry! (It'll be all right.)*

Only **nur** can be used in polite requests. It is friendly and reassuring:

Nehmen Sie **nur** Platz!	*Please take a seat.*

■ **16.3.2** In rhetorical questions (those where one doesn't expect an answer) and in real questions, **bloß/nur** intensifies the importance of what is being said:

Wie kann man **bloß/nur** so rumlaufen?	*How can anybody walk around dressed like that?*
Wie kann ich Ihnen **bloß/nur** dafür danken?	*I really don't know how to thank you.*

| Was ist **bloß/nur** mit dir los? | *What on earth is the matter with you?* |

16.4 doch

Doch is one of the most frequently used modal particles and defies neat classification.

■ **16.4.1 Doch** can occur in isolation as an answer contradicting a negative question:

| Hat er dich **nicht** angerufen? | *Didn't he call you?* |
| **Doch.** | *Yes (he did).* |

■ **16.4.2** Similarly, statements where **doch** is stressed contradict a previous statement or question:

| Sie hatte <u>**doch**</u> recht. | *She was right after all.* |
| Du warst <u>**doch**</u> neulich hier. | *You did come here recently, didn't you?* |

However, the more frequently unstressed **doch** can convey many different meanings:

- appealing for agreement

| Das war **doch** ein schöner Tag. | *That was a nice day, wasn't it?* |

- providing an explanation

| Die Geschäfte waren **doch** schon geschlossen. | *The shops were already closed.* |

- giving a reminder

| Du warst **doch** neulich noch hier. | *Don't you remember? You were here only recently.* |

- expressing disapproval

| Das kannst du **doch** nicht machen. Das ist **doch** Betrug. | *But you can't do that! That's fraud!* |

■ **16.4.3** In questions **doch** asks for confirmation or repetition:

Du hast **doch** das Gas abgedreht?	*You did turn the gas off, didn't you?*
Wie hieß **doch** dieser Film noch?	*What was that film called again?*

■ **16.4.4** In imperatives **doch** may emphasize a command or piece of advice and often conveys a sense of impatience:

Laß es **doch** bitte sein.	*Do stop it, please.*
Geh **doch** bitte zum Arzt.	*Please do go and see a doctor.*

Doch is also often used to make requests sound less harsh:

Setzen Sie sich **doch**!	*Do sit down, please.*
Nimm dir **doch** noch ein Stück Kuchen!	*Please help yourself to another piece of cake.*

■ **16.4.5** Exclamations with **doch** can express surprise:

Was das **doch** wieder geschneit hat!	*Look how much it has snowed again!*
Das ist **doch** das Letzte!	*That's really not on!*

16.5 eben

■ **16.5.1** In statements **eben** is used to restate or confirm something, often adding an explanatory note. It may also occur in isolation or at the beginning of a sentence:

Ist mir das wirklich passiert?	*Did this really happen to me?*
Du hast **eben** einen Moment die Nerven verloren.	*You just lost your nerve for a moment.*
Wir sollten gemeinsam dagegen ankämpfen.	*We should fight this together.*
Eben, deshalb organisiere ich ja ein Treffen.	*Exactly, that's why I am organizing a meeting.*

■ **16.5.2** In imperatives (mostly introduced by **dann**, *then*) **eben** states the lack of an alternative, often with a sense of frustration. It can also intensify a command:

Dann bleib **eben** zu Hause!	*You just stay at home, then!*
Dann halt dich **eben** da raus!	*Well, you just stop interfering!*

16.6 eigentlich

■ **16.6.1** In statements **eigentlich** allows the speaker to change his or her mind. A following subordinate clause with **aber** often outlines the alternative or explains the reasons. **Eigentlich** can also tone down a refusal:

Eigentlich wollte ich zu Fuß gehen, aber dann habe ich doch den Bus genommen.	*I was actually going to walk, but then I did take the bus after all.*
Sie schien **eigentlich** ganz nett, aber sie ist doch ziemlich reserviert.	*She seemed nice enough, but she's really very reserved.*
Kommst du mit?	*Are you coming along?*
Ich wollte **eigentlich** jetzt arbeiten.	*I was actually going to do some work now.*

■ **16.6.2** **Eigentlich** makes a question friendlier and less direct. In rhetorical questions it is often reproachful:

Was hast du **eigentlich** studiert?	*Can you tell me what you studied?*
Haben Sie **eigentlich** keinen Respekt vor alten Leuten?	*Don't you have any respect for elderly people?*

16.7 etwa

Etwa is used mainly in questions and implied questions. The speaker hopes that something is not the case, but fears that it may be:

Störe ich Sie **etwa**?	*I hope I'm not disturbing you?*
Hat er **etwa** gekündigt?	*He hasn't handed in his notice, has he?*
Sie glauben (doch) nicht **etwa**, daß sie daran schuld hatte.	*You surely don't believe it was her fault?*

16.8 ja

■ **16.8.1** In statements **ja** often indicates that both speakers share some common knowledge (or at least assume that they do):

Du kennst ihn **ja**.	*You know what he's like.*
Sie wohnt **ja** schon lange nicht mehr hier.	*She hasn't been living here for a long time, as you know.*

■ **16.8.2** In imperatives **ja** (like **bloß** and **nur**, 16.3) may express a warning, but can also convey reassurance:

Sei **ja** pünktlich!	*You'd better be on time!*
Mach dir **ja** keine Sorgen!	*Don't you worry!*

■ **16.8.3** In exclamations **ja** often conveys surprise:

Das hätte ich **ja** nicht gedacht! *Well, I never!*

Note that **ja** is also the affirmative particle *yes* and can be used in isolation or as a tag:

Du kommst doch morgen, **ja**?	*You are coming tomorrow, aren't you?*

16.9 mal, nun mal

■ **16.9.1** **Mal** is mainly used in commands and requests, making them friendlier and more casual:

Geh (doch) **mal** den Nachbarn fragen.	*Why don't you just go and ask the neighbour?*
Könntest du mir bitte **mal** anfassen?	*You couldn't give me a hand with this, could you?*

However, **mal** can also convey an officious, threatening tone:

Zeigen Sie **mal** Ihren Ausweis!	*Let me see your identity card!*
Komm du **mal** nach Hause!	*You just wait till you get home!*

■ **16.9.2** The combination **nun mal** is used in statements to reiterate or confirm something (compare **eben**, 16.5.1) and carries a sense of unavoidability:

Unsere Nachbarn sind **nun mal** so.	*That's just how our neighbours are.*
Damit muß man **nun mal** rechnen.	*That's what you've got to expect, I'm afraid.*

16.10 schon

■ **16.10.1** In statements about future actions or events **schon** can be either reassuring or threatening:

Wir werden das **schon** schaffen.	*Don't worry, we'll manage.*
Dich erwischen sie **schon** noch.	*They'll get you one day.*

In other statements **schon** can express agreement, with or without reservation:

Ich denke **schon**, aber ...	*Yes, I think so, but ...*
Weimar war **schon** eine Reise wert.	*Weimar was well worth a visit.*

■ **16.10.2** In imperatives **schon** conveys urgency and impatience:

Mach **schon** auf!	*Do open the door!*
Nun geh **schon** und entschuldige dich!	*Go and apologize, quickly!*

16.11 vielleicht

■ **16.11.1** In exclamations **vielleicht** serves as an intensifier:

Ich hab' **vielleicht** einen Hunger!	I'm absolutely starving!
Wir haben **vielleicht** gelacht!	We killed ourselves laughing.

■ **16.11.2** In questions **vielleicht** can be used to ask for an explanation and carries a reproachful tone:

Kannst du mir **vielleicht** sagen, warum du so spät kommst?	Can you explain to me why you are so late?
Ist das **vielleicht** dein Ernst?	You don't really mean that, do you?

In rhetorical questions it conveys irony or even sarcasm:

Bist du **vielleicht** taub?	Are you deaf or what?
Soll ich dir **vielleicht** noch die Pantoffeln bringen?	And would you like me to bring you your slippers as well?

■ **16.11.3** In commands (which can be in the form of questions) **vielleicht** has a number of meanings:

* friendly advice

Geh **vielleicht** mal zum Rechtsanwalt!	Why don't you go and see a solicitor?

* a casual invitation

Vielleicht kommst du mal vorbei!	Why don't you come and see me some time?

* indicating that the speaker would have expected a certain action, but now has to ask for it

Vielleicht hilfst du mir mal!	You could give me a hand, you know!

16.12 wohl

■ **16.12.1** In statements **wohl** expresses probability:

Sie werden jetzt **wohl** gelandet sein.	*They will probably have landed by now.*

■ **16.12.2** In questions **wohl** can signal uncertainty or express a polite request:

Ob sie **wohl** daran gedacht hat, es mitzubringen?	*I wonder whether she's remembered to bring it?*
Kann ich **wohl** mal dein Auto ausleihen?	*Do you think I could borrow your car?*

■ **16.12.3** In commands (which are mostly in the form of questions) **wohl** can intensify:

Wirst du **wohl** still halten!	*Will you keep still!*

16.13 Clusters of modal particles

In everyday speech modal particles often occur in combination with others, which usually gives them an intensifying force:

Ruf **doch mal** an!	*Do give me a call, won't you?*
Steig **doch schon mal** ein!	*Why don't you get in!*
Du hättest **ja doch wohl mal** 'Guten Tag' sagen können.	*You could <u>at least</u> have said 'hello'!*

17 Weak and strong verbs

German verbs fall into two main categories, 'weak' and 'strong' verbs.

17.1 Weak verbs

These are by far the larger category and follow a predictable pattern. The past tense is formed by adding -te to the stem (the part of the verb that is left when the infinitive ending -en or -n is removed) and the past participle ends in -t:

infinitive	present	simple past	past participle
mach**en**	er/sie/es mach**t**	er/sie/es mach**te**	gemach**t**
to make/do	he/she/it makes	he/she/it made	made

17.2 Strong verbs

Although not as numerous as weak verbs, these include some very commonly used verbs. The vowel of the stem changes in the past tense and generally in the past participle, which ends in -en or rarely in -n. Many strong verbs also have a vowel change in parts of the present tense:

infinitive	present	simple past	past participle
bleiben	er/sie/es bleibt	er/sie/es **blieb**	geblieben
to stay	he/she/it stays	he/she/it stayed	stayed
laufen	er/sie/es läuft	er/sie/es **lief**	gelaufen
to run	he/she/it runs	he/she/it ran	run

As strong verbs do not follow a predictable pattern, their forms have to be learnt. Common strong verbs are listed in 34.3.

17.3 Irregular verbs

Among both weak and strong verbs, there are some verbs with irregularities. Irregular weak verbs are sometimes called 'mixed verbs', because they take the weak endings but also have a vowel change like strong verbs. Common verbs with irregularities are listed in 34.3.

The present tense

18.1 Uses

The German present tense can refer to past, present or future actions. It may be translated by various tenses in English.

■ **18.1.1** Past action continuing up to now:

Er **wartet** hier schon seit zwei Stunden.	*He has been waiting here for two hours.*
Wir **sind** nun schon zehn Tage hier.	*We have been here for ten days now.*

■ **18.1.2** Habitual action:

Ich **arbeite** jeden Sonntag. *I work every Sunday.*

■ **18.1.3** Action in progress:

Ich **lese** gerade ein Buch. *I am reading a book.*

■ **18.1.4** Future action, where the context makes it clear that the future is referred to:

Im Oktober **geht** er zur Universität.	*He is going/will go to university in October.*

■ **18.1.5** Vivid narrative style:

Ich **komme** aus dem Urlaub und **sehe**, daß die Einbrecher alles gestohlen haben.	*I came back from my holidays to see that the burglars had stolen everything.*

18.2 Formation: weak verbs

The present tense of weak verbs is formed by adding the following endings to the verb stem:

Sing.	1. ich	mache	I	do
	2. du	machst	you	do
	3. er/sie/es	macht	he/she/it	does
Pl.	1. wir	machen	we	
	2. ihr	macht	you	} do
	3. sie/Sie	machen	they/you (formal)	

■ **18.2.1** If the verb stem ends in **-d** or **-t**, or in **-m** or **n** preceded by a consonant other than **l** or **r**, an **-e-** is inserted before the ending of the second and third persons singular and the second person plural:

arbeiten   ich arbeite, du arbeitest, er/sie/es arbeitet,
(to work)   wir arbeiten, ihr arbeitet, sie arbeiten

■ **18.2.2** If the verb stem ends in **-s**, **-ß**, **-x** or **-z**, the ending of the second person singular loses its **-s-**, so that it is identical to the third person singular:

reisen (to travel)   ich reise, du reist, er/sie/es reist

18.3 Formation: strong verbs

The present tense endings are the same as for weak verbs, but many strong verbs have a vowel change in the second and third persons singular; see 34.3.

raten   ich rate, du rätst, er/sie/es rät,
(to guess) wir raten, ihr ratet, sie raten
geben   ich gebe, du gibst, er/sie/es gibt,
(to give)   wir geben, ihr gebt, sie geben

18.4 Formation: irregularities

These types of verb have peculiarities in the present tense:
- Auxiliary verbs (**haben, sein, werden**) see 25
- Modal verbs (**können, wollen**, etc.) see 26
- Separable verbs (**abfahren, anrufen**, etc.) see 28.3
- Impersonal verbs (**es tut mir leid, es regnet**) see 29

19 The future tense

19.1 Uses

To refer to a future action German often uses the present tense (18.1). However, the future tense is used

- to emphasize future meaning, especially where this meaning would not be clear from the context:
  Meine Tochter **wird** nicht zur Universität **gehen**. *My daughter is not going to university.*

- to stress determination to do something:
  Mach dir keine Sorgen, ich **werde** das **machen**. *Don't worry, I will do it.*

- to express probability:
  Er **wird** jetzt (wohl) in New York **sein**. *He will (probably) be in New York by now.*

19.2 Formation

The future tense is formed from the present tense of **werden** and the infinitive of the verb. The infinitive is placed at the end of a simple sentence or main clause.

Singular

1. ich	**werde**		*I*	
2. du	**wirst**		*you*	
3. er/sie/es	**wird**		*he/she/it*	*will learn*
Plural		Deutsch **lernen**		*German*
1. wir	**werden**		*we*	
2. ihr	**werdet**		*you*	
3. sie/Sie	**werden**		*they/you (formal)*	

20 The past tenses: the perfect

Both the perfect tense and the simple past tense (21) refer to actions in the past. Which tense is chosen is largely a matter of personal and stylistic preference rather than of meaning. However, formal written German tends to use the simple past, while the perfect tense is more common in spoken and informal written German. Note that the perfect is not an exact equivalent of the English present perfect tense, but is often translated by the English simple past.

20.1 Uses

The perfect tense is preferred in both written and spoken German for

- a past action with continuing relevance to the present:

  Ich kann nicht arbeiten, weil ich mir das Bein **gebrochen habe**. — *I can't work because I have broken my leg.*

  Ich **habe** immer viel **gelesen**. — *I've always read a lot.*

- an action to be completed in the future:

  Wenn sie die Examen **bestanden hat**, wird sie eine Fete geben. — *When she has passed her exams she will have a party.*

- a series of repeated actions lasting up to the present:

  Wir **sind** oft in Spanien **gewesen**. — *We've often been to Spain.*

The perfect is also used in speech and informal writing for past actions with no direct link to the present, where the simple past would normally be used in more formal writing.

Sie **hat** ihre Mutter jeden Sonntag **besucht**. — *She used to visit her mother every Sunday.*

> Gestern **sind** wir in Granada **angekommen** und **haben** gleich die Alhambra **besichtigt**.

> *We arrived in Granada yesterday and immediately went to see the Alhambra.*

20.2 Formation

The perfect is formed from the present tense of **haben**, or less often **sein**, plus the past participle of the verb. The past participle is placed at the end of a simple sentence or main clause.

■ **20.2.1** Most verbs form the perfect with **haben**.

Singular

1. ich	**habe**			*I*		
2. du	**hast**			*you*		
3. er/sie/es	**hat**			*he/she/it*		

		gestern **gearbeitet**			*worked yesterday*

Plural

1. wir	**haben**			*we*		
2. ihr	**habt**			*you*		
3. sie/Sie	**haben**			*they/ you (formal)*		

■ **20.2.2** Most verbs forming the perfect with **sein** are strong verbs.

Singular

1. ich	**bin**			*I*		
2. du	**bist**			*you*		
3. er/sie/es	**ist**			*he/she/it*		

		gestern **angekommen**			*arrived yesterday*

Plural

1. wir	**sind**			*we*		
2. ihr	**seid**			*you*		
3. sie/Sie	**sind**			*they/ you (formal)*		

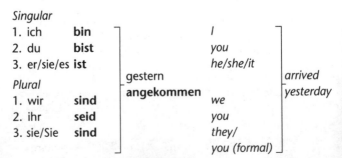

Sein is used with some common verbs which express
either a change of place or a change of state:

$$\text{Er ist nach Hause} \left\{ \begin{array}{l} \textbf{gegangen.} \\ \textbf{gefahren.} \\ \textbf{geflogen.} \end{array} \right. \qquad \text{He} \left\{ \begin{array}{l} \textit{went} \\ \textit{drove} \\ \textit{flew} \end{array} \right. \textit{home.}$$

Das Licht **ist ausgegangen.**   *The light went out.*
Sie ist gestern **gestorben.**   *She died yesterday.*

Other verbs taking **sein** include **bleiben** (*to stay*), **gelingen**
(*to succeed*), **geschehen** (*to happen*), **passieren** (*to happen*),
sein (*to be*).

20.3 Formation of the past participle

■ **20.3.1** The past participle of weak verbs is usually
formed by adding **ge-** before and **-t** after the verb stem, or
-et if the stem ends in **-d** or **-t** or in **-m** or **-n** preceded by a
consonant other than **l** or **r**:

machen *(to make)*   **ge-** + mach + -t → gemacht
reden *(to talk)*   **ge-** + red + -et → geredet
öffnen *(to open)*   **ge-** + öffn + -et → geöffnet

The **ge-** is omitted if the verb ends in **-ieren**:
telefonieren *(to phone)* telefonier + -t → telefoniert

■ **20.3.2** Strong verbs add **ge** before and **-en** after the
verb stem:
lesen *(to read)*   **ge-** + les + -en → gelesen

In many strong verbs the verb stem has vowel changes
and sometimes also consonant changes (see 34.3):
gehen *(to go)*   **ge-** + **gang** + -en → gegangen

■ **20.3.3** Irregular weak verbs (mixed verbs) add **ge-** and **-t**
like the weak verbs, but have a vowel change like many
strong verbs (see 34.3):
kennen *(to know)*   **ge-** + kann + -t → gekannt

■ **20.3.4** These types of verb have peculiarities in the formation or use of the past participle:

- The auxiliary verb **werden** see 25.1.2
- Modal verbs (**können**, **wollen**, etc.) see 26.2.2
- Compound verbs (**abfahren**, **empfehlen**, etc.) see 28.1–3

20.4 The past participle as an adjective

The past participle may be used as an adjective or an adjectival noun; it is then declined like an adjective (9.2).

- As an adjective:
  Gekochten Schinken esse ich nicht.   *I don't eat cooked ham.*

  Sie ist eine **gelehrte** Frau.   *She is an educated woman.*

- As an adjectival noun:
  Der **Beklagte** bekannte sich schuldig.   *The accused pleaded guilty.*

  Sie hat einen **Geliebten**.   *She has a lover.*

The past tenses: the simple past

The simple past is also sometimes called the 'imperfect' or simply the 'past tense'.

21.1 Uses

The simple past is the preferred tense for past actions and narratives in formal written German (e.g. business correspondence, newspaper articles):

Letzes Jahr **gab** der Staat sehr wenig für Bildung **aus.**	*Last year the state spent very little on education.*
In unserem Brief vom 8.1. **schrieben** wir Ihnen ...	*In our letter of 8/1 we wrote to you ...*

It is also used in spoken as well as written German, in preference to the perfect tense, for

- all modal verbs (26):

Er **konnte** nicht kommen.	*He couldn't come.*
Sie **mußte** für die Prüfung lernen.	*She had to study for her exam.*

- some of the most commonly used verbs, including **bleiben, gehen, haben, kommen, sein, stehen:**

Ich **blieb** bis zum späten Abend.	*I stayed until late in the evening.*
Die Studenten **kamen** und **gingen**, wie sie Lust hatten.	*The students came and went as they pleased.*

21.2 Formation: weak verbs

The simple past of weak verbs is formed by adding the following endings to the verb stem:

Sing.				
1.	ich	diskutier**te**	*I*	⎤
2.	du	diskutier**test**	*you*	⎬ *discussed*
3.	er/sie/es	diskutier**te**	*he/she/it*	⎦

Pl.	1. wir	diskutier**ten**	*we*	
	2. ihr	diskutier**tet**	*you*	*discussed*
	3. sie/Sie	diskutier**ten**	*they/you (formal)*	

If the verb stem ends in **-d** or **-t**, or in **-m** or **-n** preceded by a consonant other than **l** or **r**, for ease of pronunciation an **-e** is inserted between the stem and the ending in all persons:

arbeiten (*to work*)   → ich arbeit**e**te, du arbeit**e**test, ...
öff**n**en (*to open*)   → ich öffn**e**te, du öffn**e**test, ...

21.3 Formation: strong verbs

In the simple past the stem of most strong verbs has a vowel change and sometimes also a consonant change (see 34.3). The following endings are added to the past tense stem:

Sing.	1. ich	trank	*I*	
	2. du	trank**st**	*you*	
	3. er/sie/es	trank	*he/she/it*	
Pl.	1. wir	trank**en**	*we*	*drank*
	2. ihr	trank**t**	*you*	
	3. sie/Sie	trank**en**	*they/you (formal)*	

If the verb stem ends in **-s**, **-ß**, **-x** or **-z**, the ending of the second person singular (**du**) loses its **-s-** (as in the present tense, 18.2.2):

lesen (*to read*)   → ich las, du las**t**, er/sie/es las
essen (*to eat*)   → ich aß, du aß**t**, er/sie/es aß

21.4 Formation: modal and separable verbs

- For the simple past of modal verbs see 26.2.2.
- For the simple past of separable verbs (**abfahren**, **anrufen**, etc.) see 28.3.1.

The past tenses: the pluperfect

22.1 Use

The pluperfect is used to refer to an action which ended before another event in the past:

Er fuhr mit dem Taxi nach Hause, weil er den Bus **verpaßt hatte**.

He went home by taxi because he had missed the bus.

Als sie eine halbe Stunde **gewartet hatte**, ging sie alleine ins Kino.

After she had waited for half an hour, she went to the cinema on her own.

22.2 Formation

The pluperfect is formed from the simple past of **haben** or **sein** and the past participle of the verb. The past participle is placed at the end of a simple sentence or main clause. For the use of **haben** or **sein** and the formation of the past participle see 20.2–3.

■ 22.2.1 Pluperfect with **haben**

Sing.	1. ich	**hatte**		I	
	2. du	**hattest**		you	
	3. er/sie/es	**hatte**	geschlafen	he/she/it	had slept
Pl.	1. wir	**hatten**		we	
	2. ihr	**hattet**		you	
	3. sie/Sie	**hatten**		they/you	

■ 22.2.2 Pluperfect with **sein**

Sing.	1. ich	**war**		I	
	2. du	**warst**		you	
	3. er/sie/es	**war**	gegangen	he/she/it	had gone
Pl.	1. wir	**waren**		we	
	2. ihr	**wart**		you	
	3. sie/Sie	**waren**		they/you	

The passive

The terms 'active voice' and 'passive voice' refer to the relationship between the verb and its subject.

Whereas in the active voice the subject of the verb carries out the action, in the passive voice the subject of the verb is the receiver of the action.

active	passive
Ich verkaufe mein Auto.	**Mein Auto** wird verkauft.
I'm selling my car.	*My car is being sold.*

The passive is used less frequently in German than in English, but passive constructions do occur in speech and are often found in journalism and in commercial, official and legal documents.

23.1 Uses

The passive is used in order to emphasize the action itself rather than the person or thing (the 'agent') which causes it. Often the agent is not mentioned, or is unknown.

Das Büro wird morgen gestrichen.	*The office will be painted tomorrow.*
Ab 1. Januar werden die Preise erhöht.	*The prices will be increased as of 1st January.*

A characteristic and common use of the passive is in impersonal constructions; see 29.2.

23.2 Formation

■ **23.2.1** The present passive is formed from the present tense of **werden** and the past participle of the verb, which is placed at the end of a simple sentence or main clause.

Sing.	1. ich	**werde**		*I am*	
	2. du	**wirst**	**gerufen**	*you are*	*called*
	3. er/sie/es	**wird**		*he/she/it is*	

Pl.	1. wir	**werden**		*we are*	
	2. ihr	**werdet**	gerufen	*you are*	called
	3. sie/Sie	**werden**		*they/you (formal) are*	

■ **23.2.2** The future passive is formed from the future tense of **werden** and the past participle of the verb. The infinitive of **werden** is placed at the end of a simple sentence or main clause, following the past participle.

  Ich **werde gerufen**   *I will be called.*
  werden.

■ **23.2.3** The simple past passive is formed from the simple past tense of **werden** and the past participle of the verb, which is placed at the end of a simple sentence or main clause.

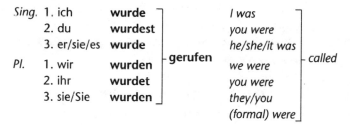

Sing.	1. ich	**wurde**		*I was*	
	2. du	**wurdest**		*you were*	
	3. er/sie/es	**wurde**	gerufen	*he/she/it was*	called
Pl.	1. wir	**wurden**		*we were*	
	2. ihr	**wurdet**		*you were*	
	3. sie/Sie	**wurden**		*they/you (formal) were*	

■ **23.2.4** The perfect and pluperfect passive are formed from the perfect/pluperfect of **werden** (25.1.2) and the past participle of the verb. **Worden** is placed at the end of a simple sentence or main clause, following the past participle.

- perfect passive
  Ich **bin gerufen worden.**   *I have been called.*

- pluperfect passive
  Ich **war gerufen worden.**   *I had been called.*

23.3 The agent

The equivalent of the English *by*, which indicates the agent of an action (the person or thing which causes it), is **von**, **durch** or **mit** in German.

- **von** + dative is generally used for persons:

  Die Berliner Mauer wurde **von** den Kommunisten gebaut.　*The Berlin Wall was built by the Communists.*

- **durch** + accusative is most frequently used for things:

  Berlin wurde **durch** die Mauer geteilt.　*Berlin was divided by the Wall.*

However, in many cases **von** and **durch** are interchangeable:

  Das Haus wurde **durch** ein/ **von** einem Feuer zerstört.　*The house was destroyed by a fire.*

- **mit** + dative is used for instruments:

  Der Brief wurde **mit** der Hand geschrieben.　*The letter was written by hand.*

23.4 The descriptive passive

Much less common is the passive formed with **sein** (known as the **Zustandspassiv**). This emphasizes the state resulting from an action rather than the action itself. It is rarely used other than in the present and simple past.

*'normal' passive (**werden**)*	*descriptive passive (**sein**)*
Die Küche **wird** geputzt. *The kitchen is being cleaned.*	Die Küche **ist** geputzt. *The kitchen is clean.*
Berlin **wurde** 1945 von den Russen besetzt. *The Russians occupied Berlin in 1945.*	Berlin **war** 1945 von den Russen besetzt. *In 1945 Berlin was under Russian occupation.*

23.5 Alternatives to the passive

In everyday German there is a strong tendency to avoid the passive voice, and there are many alternative constructions.

■ **23.5.1** The impersonal pronoun **man** (*one*) as an indefinite subject:

Man kann Deutsch nicht in einer Woche lernen.	*German can't be learnt in a week.*
Hier spricht **man** Französisch.	*French is spoken here.*

■ **23.5.2** Reflexive verbs:

Das Geld wird **sich** sicher **wiederfinden**.	*I'm sure the money will be found.*

■ **23.5.3** sich lassen + infinitive instead of a passive with **können**:

Das **läßt sich** nicht vermeiden.	*It can't be avoided.*

■ **23.5.4** An infinitive phrase with **sein + zu** instead of a passive with **können** or **müssen**:

Das **ist** nicht bis Montag **zu** schaffen.	*This can't be done by Monday.*

■ **23.5.5** erhalten, bekommen, kriegen (in order of decreasing formality):

Er erhält/bekommt/kriegt die Goldmedaille.	*He is awarded the gold medal.*

The subjunctive mood

The 'mood' of a verb indicates the speaker's attitude towards what is said. The indicative mood (covered in sections 18 to 23) describes an action or a state as factual, true or at least possible. The subjunctive mood is used to express something which is unreal, hypothetical or not necessarily true. The subjunctive occurs in informal as well as formal German, and its use differs considerably from the use of the subjunctive in English.

24.1 Konjunktiv I and II

There are two types of subjunctive in German: **Konjunktiv I** and **Konjunktiv II**. **Konjunktiv I** is used mainly in indirect speech, whereas **Konjunktiv II** expresses hypothetical or imaginary concepts and actions. Both types exist in various tenses.

24.2 Konjunktiv II Gegenwart: formation

This, the 'base' tense of Konjunktiv II, is also referred to as the 'past subjunctive'. It has two alternative forms: the two-word construction and the one-word form. The meaning of both is the same, and the choice of one or the other is largely a matter of style.

■ **24.2.1** The two-word construction is the more common form and is generally used for all verbs apart from **haben**, **sein**, **werden** and the modal verbs, particularly in everyday language. It is formed from the **Konjunktiv II Gegenwart** of **werden** plus the infinitive of the verb.

Sing.					
1. ich	**würde**		*I*		
2. du	**würdest**	**gehen**	*you*		*would go*
3. er/sie/es	**würde**		*he/she/it*		

Pl.	1. wir	**würden**		we	
	2. ihr	**würdet**	gehen	you	would go
	3. sie/Sie	**würden**		they/you (formal)	

■ **24.2.2** The one-word **Konjunktiv II Gegenwart** is derived from the simple past of the indicative, as follows.

a For weak verbs it is identical to the regular simple past (21.2). It is used only in formal language.

Und wenn Sie mehr Geld **verdienten**?	*And if you were earning more money?*

Compare the simple past:

Sie sind nur geblieben, weil Sie mehr Geld **verdienten**?	*You only stayed because you were earning more money?*

b For irregular weak verbs (mixed verbs) it is the same as the simple past, but with an Umlaut or vowel change.

Infinitive	Simple past	Konjunktiv II
denken (*to think*)	ich dachte	ich dächte
rennen (*to run*)	ich rannte	ich rennte

c For strong verbs it is formed from the simple past by adding an Umlaut to the past tense stem of the verb where appropriate and adding the endings -e, -est, -e, -en, -et, -en. Some strong verbs are frequently used in the one-word form, including:

finden (*to find*): ich fände
geben (*to give*): ich gäbe
gehen (*to go*): ich ginge
halten (*to hold*): ich hielte
heißen (*to be called*): ich hieße

kommen (*to come*): ich käme
lassen (*to leave*): ich ließe
sehen (*to see*): ich sähe
tun (*to do*): ich täte
wissen (*to know*): ich wüßte

The one-word form is often used to avoid two **würde** constructions in one sentence:

Ich **fände** es schön, wenn *I'd like it very much if you* du mitkommen würdest. *came with me.*

d For the one-word **Konjunktiv II Gegenwart** of **haben**, **sein**, **werden** and the modal verbs see 25.3 and 26.2.2.

24.3 Konjunktiv II Vergangenheit: formation

This is also referred to as the 'pluperfect subjunctive'. It consists of the **Konjunktiv II Gegenwart** forms of **haben** or **sein** (see 25.3) plus the past participle of the verb.

Wir **hätten** dir gern *We would have liked to help* **geholfen**. *you.*
Sie **wäre** länger **geblieben**, *She would have stayed longer* wenn du **gekommen** *if you had come.* **wärst**.

24.4 Konjunktiv II: uses

■ **24.4.1** Hypothetical statements:

Er **wäre** glücklich, wenn *He would be happy if she* sie hier **wäre**. *were here.*
Wenn ich das **gewußt** *If I had known this, I wouldn't* **hätte**, **wäre** ich nicht *have come.* **gekommen**.

Wenn can sometimes be omitted. The sentence then normally begins with the subordinate clause, with the verb preceding the subject. The following main clause is usually introduced by **dann** or **so**.

Würdest du nur weniger *If only you smoked less, you* **rauchen**, dann **hättest** *would have more of an* du mehr Appetit. *appetite.*

■ **24.4.2** Wishes:

Ich **wünschte**, ich **hätte** mehr Zeit für dich.	*I wish I had more time for you.*
Ich **wäre** gern noch länger **geblieben**.	*I would have liked to stay longer.*

■ **24.4.3** Polite requests:

Würden Sie mir bitte die Butter **reichen**?	*Would you pass the butter, please?*
Hätten Sie heute Zeit?	*Would you have some time today?*

■ **24.4.4** Speculation and doubt:

Sie **könnten** nun in New York gelandet sein.	*They could have landed in New York by now.*
Wir waren unsicher, ob du noch **kommen würdest**.	*We weren't sure whether you'd come after all.*

24.5 Konjunktiv I: formation

■ **24.5.1** **Konjunktiv I Gegenwart** is also referred to as the 'present subjunctive'. It is formed by adding **-e, -est, -e, -en, -et, -en** to the verb stem.

Er sagt, er **lese** das Buch.   *He says he is reading the book.*

■ **24.5.2** **Konjunktiv I Zukunft** is also known as the 'future subjunctive'. It is formed from the **Konjunktiv I Gegenwart** of **werden** plus the infinitive.

Er sagte, er **werde** das Buch **lesen**.   *He said he would read the book.*

■ **24.5.3** **Konjunktiv I Vergangenheit** is also referred to as the 'perfect subjunctive'. It is formed from the **Konjunktiv I Gegenwart** of **haben** or **sein** plus the past participle.

Er sagte, er **habe** das Buch **gelesen**.   *He said he had read the book.*

24.6 Konjunktiv I: use

German uses **Konjunktiv I** to express indirect speech in formal language:

Der Spiegel berichtete, die Rezession in Deutschland **sei** vorüber.	*The 'Spiegel' reported that the recession in Germany was over.*

■ **24.6.1** The following table shows how the different tenses of the subjunctive are used for indirect speech.

Direct speech (indicative)	Indirect speech (subjunctive)
present	→ *present*
Sie **liest** das Buch. *She is reading the book.*	Sie sagt, sie **lese** das Buch. *She says she is reading the book.* Sie sagte, sie **lese** das Buch. *She said she was reading the book.*
future	→ *future*
Sie **wird** das Buch lesen. *She will read the book.*	Sie sagt, sie **werde** das Buch **lesen**. *She says she will read the book.* Sie sagte, sie **werde** das Buch **lesen**. *She said she would read the book.*
simple past/perfect/pluperfect	→ *perfect*
Sie **las** das Buch. *She read the book.* Sie **hat** das Buch **gelesen**. *She has read the book.* Sie **hatte** das Buch **gelesen**. *She had read the book.*	Sie sagt, sie **habe** das Buch **gelesen**. *She says she has read the book.* Sie sagte, sie **habe** das Buch **gelesen**. *She said she had read the book.*

■ **24.6.2** The exception to the above pattern is that, where the **Konjunktiv I** form would be identical with the present indicative, it is always replaced by **Konjunktiv II**:

Er behauptete, Sie **spielten** kein Golf.	*He maintained you did not play golf.*
Ich kündigte an, daß ich den Empfang in der Botschaft **gäbe**.	*I announced that I would give the reception in the embassy.*

■ **24.6.3** In colloquial language **Konjunktiv I** is almost entirely avoided and is replaced by either the present indicative or **Konjunktiv II** (one-word form):

Mein Freund hat gesagt, die Rezession **ist/wäre** vorbei.	*My friend said that the recession was over.*
Im Fernsehen haben sie gesagt, der Rhein **hat/ hätte** wieder Hochwasser.	*They said on the TV that the Rhine had flooded again.*
Er hat mir versprochen, er **wird/würde** es versuchen.	*He promised me that he would give it a try.*

25 Auxiliary verbs: haben, sein, werden

Auxiliary verbs 'help' other verbs to form their tenses. The three main auxiliary verbs in German are **haben** (*to have*), **sein** (*to be*) and **werden** (*to become*).

25.1 Use as auxiliaries

■ **25.1.1** **Haben** and **sein** are used as auxiliaries to form the perfect and pluperfect tenses (20 and 22). Most verbs form these tenses with **haben** plus the past participle of the verb. For the verbs which use **sein** see 20.2.2.

Wir **haben** noch nicht **gegessen**.	*We haven't eaten yet.*
Sie **ist** in die Stadt **gegangen**.	*She went into town.*
Sie **hatte** eine Stunde gewartet.	*She had waited for one hour.*
Ich **war** die ganze Zeit hier **gewesen**.	*I had been here all the time.*

■ **25.1.2** **Werden** is used to form the following:

* Future tense (19.2): present tense of **werden** plus the infinitive of the verb

Ich **werde** mich jetzt auf den Weg **machen**.	*I'll be on my way now.*

* Passive voice (23.2): appropriate tense of **werden** plus the past participle of the verb

Das Büro **wird** gerade **gesäubert**.	*The office is being cleaned at the moment.*

When **werden** is used as a passive auxiliary the special form **worden** is used instead of the past participle **geworden**:

Er **ist** gerade **operiert worden**.	*He has just been operated on.*

- **Konjunktiv II Gegenwart (24.2.1): Konjunktiv II Gegenwart** of **werden** plus the infinitive of the verb

Ich **würde** gerne etwas essen.	*I would like to eat something.*

25.2 Non-auxiliary use

All three verbs can also be used without another verb. In this case they no longer have an auxiliary function:

Ich **habe** nicht viel Geld.	*I haven't got a lot of money.*
Ich **bin** Student.	*I'm a student.*
Sie ist Lehrerin **geworden**.	*She became a teacher.*

25.3 Formation

Haben, **sein** and **werden** are all irregular verbs. The most commonly used forms are set out below.

			haben	sein	werden
Present tense					
Sing.	1.	ich	habe	bin	werde
	2.	du	hast	bist	wirst
	3.	er/sie/es	hat	ist	wird
Pl.	1.	wir	haben	sind	werden
	2.	ihr	habt	seid	werdet
	3.	sie/Sie	haben	sind	werden
Simple past					
Sing.	1.	ich	hatte	war	wurde
	2.	du	hattest	warst	wurdest
	3.	er/sie/es	hatte	war	wurde
Pl.	1.	wir	hatten	waren	wurden
	2.	ihr	hattet	wart	wurdet
	3.	sie/Sie	hatten	waren	wurden

		haben	sein	werden
Konjunktiv II Gegenwart				
Sing.	1. ich	hätte	wäre	würde
	2. du	hättest	wärest	würdest
	3. er/sie/es	hätte	wäre	würde
Pl.	1. wir	hätten	wären	würden
	2. ihr	hättet	wäret	würdet
	3. sie/Sie	hätten	wären	würden
Perfect				
	1. ich etc.	habe etc. gehabt	bin etc. gewesen	bin etc. (ge)worden

There are six modal verbs (or modal auxiliaries) in German, which can express a wide range of meanings beyond their literal English translations: **dürfen** (*to be allowed to*), **können** (*to be able to*), **mögen** (*to like*), **müssen** (*to have to*), **sollen** (*ought to*), **wollen** (*to want*). Their main function is to express the speaker's attitude, such as a liking for something, an obligation, or an ability to do something.

26.1 Uses

■ **26.1.1** Modal verbs are normally used with another verb, which appears in the infinitive at the end of a simple sentence or main clause:

Darf ich hier **rauchen**?	*May I smoke here?*
Ich **möchte** nächstes Jahr nach Österreich **fahren**.	*I would like to go to Austria next year.*
Du **mußt** sofort **kommen**.	*You must come immediately.*

Verbs expressing motion and the verbs **tun** and **machen** are often omitted when a modal verb is used:

Ich **konnte** leider nicht früher (**kommen**).	*I'm afraid I couldn't come any earlier.*
Mußt du das wirklich (**machen**)?	*Do you really have to do this?*

■ **26.1.2** The **Konjunktiv II** forms of modal verbs (26.2.2) are often used to convey politeness:

Dürfte ich mal eben telefonieren?	*Could I just use your phone?*
Möchten Sie den Anzug anprobieren?	*Would you like to try on the suit?*
Sie **müßten** das noch erledigen.	*You ought to finish that.*

■ **26.1.3** Individual uses of modal verbs

a Können expresses ability, possibility and, in colloquial language, also permission (as an alternative to **dürfen**):

Ich **kann** nicht aufstehen, ich habe mir das Bein gebrochen.	*I can't stand up, I've broken my leg.*
Ich **kann** dir dabei helfen.	*I can help you with that.*
Kann ich hier rauchen?	*May I smoke here?*

b Müssen expresses necessity or certainty:

Wir **müssen** einen neuen Computer kaufen.	*We have to buy a new computer.*
Das **muß** an der Sicherung liegen.	*It must be the fuse.*

Note that **nicht müssen** is equivalent to 'need not' or 'doesn't have to' in English (not 'must not'):

Sie **muß** heute **nicht** ins Büro.	*She doesn't need to go to the office today.*

c Dürfen usually expresses permission. In its **Konjunktiv II** form (**dürfte**) it can add politeness or suggest probability:

Darf (Dürfte) ich das Fenster öffnen?	*May I open (Would you mind if I opened) the window?*
Sie **dürfte** schon zu Hause sein.	*She ought to be home by now.*

The negative **nicht dürfen** is equivalent to 'must not':

Sie **dürfen** hier **nicht** rauchen.	*You mustn't smoke here.*

d Mögen generally expresses liking. In contrast to other modal verbs, it often occurs without another verb:

Ich **mag** gern Süßes.	*I like sweet things.*

In its **Konjunktiv II** form **möchte**, either with or without another verb, it expresses a wish or request:

Ich **möchte** dieses Kleid.	*I'd like this dress.*
Wir **möchten** jetzt zu Abend **essen**.	*We'd like to have our dinner now.*

Mögen can also express possibility and polite indirect requests:

Er **mag** wohl um die vierzig sein.	*He may well be about forty.*
Er sagte ihr, sie **möchte** schon mal Platz nehmen.	*He invited her to take a seat.*

e **Sollen** is used to express advice, obligation, a supposition or an intention:

Der Arzt hat gesagt, ich **soll** im Bett bleiben.	*The doctor said I should stay in bed.*
Soll ich dir eine Kopf- schmerztablette holen?	*Shall I get you a headache tablet?*
Sie **soll** sehr krank gewesen sein.	*She is supposed to have been very ill.*
Das **sollte** eine Überraschung sein.	*That was meant to be a surprise.*

f **Wollen** usually indicates a strong wish, like *want*. It may also express a polite suggestion, a claim or a necessity:

Er **will** sein Auto verkaufen.	*He wants to sell his car.*
Wollen wir nicht noch bei Peter vorbeigehen?	*Why don't we drop in at Peter's?*
Er **will** Experte auf diesem Gebiet sein.	*He claims to be an expert in this field.*
Das **will** geübt sein.	*That needs to be practised.*

26.2 Formation

Unlike their English counterparts, German modal verbs can be used in all tenses. They have irregular present tenses and some have vowel/consonant changes in other tenses.

■ 26.2.1 Present tense

	wollen	mögen	müssen	dürfen	sollen	können
Sing.						
1. ich	will	mag	muß	darf	soll	kann
2. du	willst	magst	mußt	darfst	sollst	kannst
3. er	will	mag	muß	darf	soll	kann
Plural						
1. wir	wollen	mögen	müssen	dürfen	sollen	können
2. ihr	wollt	mögt	müßt	dürft	sollt	könnt
3. sie	wollen	mögen	müssen	dürfen	sollen	können

■ 26.2.2 Summary of other tenses

Infinitive		*Simple past*	*Konjunktiv II*	*Perfect*
wollen	ich	wollte	wollte	habe ... gewollt/wollen
mögen	ich	mochte	möchte	habe ... gemocht/mögen
müssen	ich	mußte	müßte	habe ... gemußt/müssen
dürfen	ich	durfte	dürfte	habe ... gedurft/dürfen
sollen	ich	sollte	sollte	habe ... gesollt/sollen
können	ich	konnte	könnte	habe ... gekonnt/können

The past participle form with **ge-** is only used when the modal is used without another verb:

Er hat das nicht **ge**wollt.　　*He didn't intend that.*

The modal infinitive is used instead if there is another verb. In this 'double infinitive' construction the modal infinitive always follows the other verb:

Ich habe das kaufen **wollen**.　　*I wanted to buy it.*
Du hättest das wissen **müssen**. *You should have known that.*

In modern German these rather complicated perfect tense forms are usually replaced by the much shorter simple past.

Ich **wollte** das kaufen.　　*I wanted to buy it.*

Reflexive verbs

Reflexive verbs are verbs with a pronoun in the accusative or dative which refers back to the subject of the sentence.

Ich wasche **mich.**	*I wash (myself).*
Ich merke **mir** das.	*I remember that.*

German has a large number of reflexive verbs, many of which do not have a reflexive equivalent in English. In a dictionary, the infinitive is given with the reflexive pronoun **sich**.

27.1 Formation

Reflexive verbs may be weak, strong or mixed. For the formation of the tenses see 34. The perfect tense of reflexive verbs is normally formed with **haben**.

27.2 Accusative/Dative reflexive pronouns

The reflexive pronoun may be either the direct object of the verb (therefore in the accusative case) or the indirect object (dative case).

■ **27.2.1** Reflexive verb + accusative
The majority of reflexive verbs follow this pattern.

Sing.	1. ich	wasche **mich**	*I'm*		*myself*
	2. du	wäschst **dich**	*you are*		*yourself*
	3. er/sie/es	wäscht **sich**	*he/she/ it is*		*himself/ herself/ itself*
				washing	
Pl.	1. wir	waschen **uns**	*we are*		*ourselves*
	2. ihr	wascht **euch**	*you are*		*yourselves*
	3. sie/Sie	waschen **sich**	*they/ you are*		*themselves/ yourself*

Some frequently used verbs in this category are:

sich anziehen	*to get dressed*
sich ärgern (über)	*to get annoyed (about/with)*
sich aufregen (über)	*to get excited/annoyed (about)*
sich ausziehen	*to undress*
sich bedanken (für)	*to say thank you (for)*
sich beeilen	*to hurry*
sich beschäftigen (mit)	*to occupy oneself (with)*
sich erinnern (an)	*to remember*
sich freuen (über/auf)	*to be pleased (about)/to look forward (to)*
sich fürchten (vor)	*to be afraid (of)*
sich gewöhnen (an)	*to get used (to)*
sich interessieren (für)	*to be interested (in)*
sich nähern	*to get close (to)*
sich rasieren	*to shave*
sich setzen	*to sit down*
sich umsehen	*to look around*
sich unterhalten (über/mit)	*to talk (about/with)*
sich verabschieden	*to say goodbye*

Some of these verbs, such as **sich anziehen**, **sich rasieren**, **sich waschen**, can also take a direct object. The accusative pronoun changes to the dative when there is a direct object:

Ich ziehe **mich** an.	*I'm getting dressed.*
Ich ziehe **mir** den Mantel an.	*I'm putting on my coat.*
Wäschst du **dich**?	*Are you washing yourself?*
Wäschst du **dir** den Hals?	*Are you washing your neck?*

■ **27.2.2** Reflexive verb + dative

A small group of verbs are used with reflexive pronouns in the dative case. These are **mir** and **dir** for the first and second person singular. The other forms are identical to the accusative:

Sing.	1. ich	merke **mir**		*I*	*remember*	
	2. du	merkst **dir**		*you*	*remember*	
	3. er/sie/es	merkt **sich**		*he/she/it*	*remembers*	
			-das			-that
Pl.	1. wir	merken **uns**		*we*	*remember*	
	2. ihr	merkt **euch**		*you*	*remember*	
	3. sie/Sie	merken **sich**		*they/you*	*remember*	

The most common verbs in this group are:

sich (etwas) abgewöhnen	*to give up (sthg)*
sich aneignen	*to appropriate/learn*
sich ansehen	*to have a look at*
sich besorgen	*to get/buy for oneself*
sich einbilden	*to imagine*
sich erlauben	*to allow oneself*
sich kaufen	*to buy for oneself*
sich leisten	*to afford*
sich (etwas) merken	*to remember (sthg)*
sich vornehmen	*to plan, to undertake*
sich vorstellen	*to imagine*
sich wünschen	*to want*

28 Compound verbs

Compound verbs consist of a verb with a prefix attached to it, e.g. *miß*verstehen (*to misunderstand*) or *wieder*sehen (*to see again*). German has many more compound verbs than English.

There are three categories of prefixes: separable, inseparable and variable (i.e. those which are sometimes separable and sometimes inseparable). It is helpful to concentrate first on the two latter categories, in which there are only a limited number of prefixes to be learnt.

28.1 Inseparable prefixes

The following seven prefixes are inseparable: **be-, emp-, ent-, er-, ge-, ver-, zer-**. In speech, verbs with these prefixes ('inseparable verbs') always have the main stress on the verb and not on the prefix. Examples:

bekommen	Ich **bekomme** einen Tee.	*I'll have a cup of tea.*
entschuldigen	Sie **entschuldigt** sich.	*She gives her apologies.*
gefallen	Das Bild **gefällt** mir.	*I like the picture.*
verstehen	Das **verstehe** ich.	*I understand that.*

Verbs with inseparable or double inseparable prefixes (e.g. **anver**trauen – *to entrust*) form the past participle without **ge-**:

Sie hat den Wein **empfohlen**. *She recommended the wine.*
Sie haben uns das **anvertraut**. *They entrusted us with it.*

28.2 Variable prefixes

The following prefixes may be separable or inseparable: **durch-, hinter-, miß-, über-, um-, unter, voll-, wider-, wieder-**:

untergehen *(sep.)*	unternehmen *(insep.)*
Das Schiff **geht unter**.	Er **unternimmt** eine Reise.
The ship is sinking.	*He is going on a journey.*

The same prefix may be used with the same verb both as a separable and as an inseparable prefix. The meaning of the two resulting verbs is different; the separable verb is often used in a literal sense, whereas the inseparable verb is used in a figurative sense:

<u>wie</u>derholen (separable, stress on **wieder**)	wieder<u>ho</u>len (inseparable, stress on **holen**)
Ich **hole** dir den Ball **wieder**. I'll bring you the ball back.	Ich **wiederhole** die Frage. I'll repeat the question.

For the formation of the tenses of separable verbs see 28.3.

28.3 Separable prefixes

All prefixes other than those mentioned in 28.1 and 28.2 are separable. In speech the main stress is on the prefix. These prefixes are derived from other parts of speech, such as prepositions (**mitkommen** – to come along), adjectives (**freisprechen** – to acquit), adverbs (**festhalten** – to hold on to), nouns (**teilnehmen** – to take part) and verbs (**stehenbleiben** – to stand still).

■ **28.3.1** In the simple tenses and the imperative the prefix is normally separated from the verb and placed at the end of the clause:

Er **ruft** gerade einen Freund **an**.	He is just phoning a friend.
Sie **rief** gestern **an**.	She called yesterday.
Ruf mich bitte später **an**.	Please call me later.

But in subordinate clauses where the verb is placed at the end, the prefix remains attached to the verb:

| Ich hoffe, daß er gut **ankommt**. | I hope that he will arrive safely. |

■ **28.3.2** In the compound tenses the prefix is never separated from the verb:

Ich werde morgen **anrufen**. — *I'm going to phone tomorrow.*

Der Angeklagte wurde **freigesprochen**. — *The accused was acquitted.*

In the past participle the **-ge-** is inserted after the prefix:

Das Tier hat meine Bewegungen nach**ge**ahmt. — *The animal imitated my movements.*

Ich habe es nach**ge**schlagen. — *I looked it up.*

■ **28.3.3** In infinitive constructions with **zu**, the **zu** is inserted after the prefix:

Ich habe vergessen, es **nachzuschlagen**. — *I forgot to look it up.*

Impersonal verbs are used with the impersonal pronoun **es** (*it*) either as the true subject of the clause or as a substitute for a subject.

29.1 es as a true subject

■ **29.1.1** In the following constructions **es** is the only possible subject and can never be left out. The English equivalent is usually a construction with *it* or a personal verb.

- expressions of time and weather
es ist sechs Uhr	*it's six o'clock*
es regnet/schneit/friert	*it's raining/snowing/freezing*

- constructions with **gehen**
Wie **geht es** dir?	*How are you?*
Mit dem Zug **geht es** schneller.	*It's quicker by train.*

- the expression **es gibt** (+ accusative)
Es gibt hier ein Problem.	*There's a problem.*
Was **gibt's** denn?	*What's the matter?*
Da **gibt's** nichts zu lachen!	*This is not a laughing matter.*

- others
es fragt sich, ob	*the question is whether*
es handelt sich um	*it's about*
es hängt davon ab (ob)	*it depends (on whether)*
es kommt auf ... an	*it depends on ...*
es macht nichts	*it doesn't matter*

■ **29.1.2** In the following constructions **es** can be omitted if another word or phrase takes the initial position ('inversion': see 36.1.2):

Es ärgert mich, daß er immer zu spät kommt.	*It annoys me that he is always late.*

Inversion: **Mich ärgert**, daß ...

es enttäuscht mich *I'm disappointed*	es gefällt mir *I'm pleased*
es erstaunt mich *I'm astonished*	es interessiert mich *I'm interested*
es freut mich *I'm glad*	es tut mir leid *I'm sorry*
	es wundert mich *I'm surprised*

The **es** is normally dropped in the following expressions:

mir ist kalt/warm (es ist mir kalt/warm)	*I'm cold/warm*
mir ist schlecht/übel (es ist mir schlecht/übel)	*I'm feeling sick*
da fällt mir ein/mir fällt ein	*it occurs to me*

29.2 es as a substitute subject

Es may be placed at the beginning of a clause in order to emphasize the true subject. In these cases English uses expressions like *there is/are*:

Es kommen 200 Gäste.   *There are 200 guests coming.*
(Instead of: 200 Gäste kommen.)

es bleiben	*there remain*
es gehen	*there are ... going*
es ist/sind	*there is/are*

Es also occasionally replaces the 'true subject', mainly in passive and reflexive constructions. English generally prefers an active construction, often with *we, you* or *people*.

Es wurde viel **gegessen**.   *People ate a lot.*
(Instead of: Die Leute aßen viel.)

Es ließ sich nichts mehr machen.   *There was nothing more that could be done.*
(Instead of: Wir konnten nichts mehr machen.)

However, **es** can be omitted if another word or phrase takes the initial position:

Gestern wurde viel gegessen.   *People ate a lot yesterday.*

Hier darf nicht geraucht werden.   *You are not allowed to smoke here.*

Verbs and cases

Both English and German have transitive and intransitive verbs (marked in most dictionaries as *v.t.* and *v.i.* respectively). Transitive verbs can take a direct object, whereas intransitive verbs cannot.

30.1 Verbs + accusative object

Most German verbs can take a direct object in the accusative:

| Ich esse **einen Salat**. | *I'll have a salad.* |
| Jetzt lesen wir **den Roman**. | *Now we'll read the novel.* |

30.2 Verbs + dative and accusative objects

Some verbs can take two objects: an indirect object (in the dative) and a direct object (in the accusative):

| Wir bieten **unseren Kunden** *(dat.)* **einen exzellenten Service** *(acc.)*. | *We offer our customers excellent service.* |

The most common verbs normally used with two objects are:

(an)bieten	*to offer*	mitteilen	*to inform*
bringen	*to bring*	schenken	*to give*
beweisen	*to prove*		*(as a present)*
empfehlen	*to recommend*	schicken	*to send*
erzählen	*to tell*	schreiben	*to write*
geben	*to give*	schulden	*to owe*
gönnen	*to grant*	verkaufen	*to sell*
kaufen	*to buy*	zeigen	*to show*
leihen	*to lend*		

30.3 Verbs + dative object

Some German verbs can only take an object in the dative. The construction is in most cases quite different from the English equivalent.

Dieser Film gefällt **mir** gut. *I like this film.*
Es gelang **ihr**, die Arbeit   *She succeeded in completing*
fertigzustellen.   *the work.*

The most common verbs with a dative object are:

antworten	*to answer*	helfen	*to help*
begegnen	*to encounter*	imponieren	*to impress*
danken	*to thank*	mißtrauen	*to distrust*
fehlen	*to be missing*	nachgehen	*to investigate*
gefallen	*to please*	schaden	*to harm/damage*
gehören	*to belong to*	trauen	*to trust*
gelingen	*to succeed/ be successful*	vorangehen	*to precede/lead*
		weh tun	*to hurt*
gleichen	*to resemble*	widersprechen	*to contradict*
gratulieren	*to congratulate*	widerstehen	*to resist*

30.4 Verbs + genitive object

Only a few verbs – mostly used in formal speech – take an object in the genitive:

Er bediente sich **der**   *He used corruption to avoid*
Korruption, um der Strafe *punishment.*
zu entgehen.

The most common verbs normally used in this way are:

sich bedienen	*to use*
bedürfen	*to require*
sich erfreuen	*to enjoy*
gedenken	*to commemorate*
sich bemächtigen	*to take possession of*
sich erinnern	*to remember*
sich rühmen	*to boast*
sich schämen	*to be ashamed of*

30.5 Verbs + nominative complement

A small group of verbs have a complement which is
identical with the subject of the sentence and is therefore
in the nominative case:

Mein Bruder ist **ein ausgezeichneter Pianist**.	*My brother is an excellent pianist.*
Das wird **der Briefträger** sein.	*That will be the postman.*
Sie ist und bleibt **ein Genie**.	*She is and always will be a genius.*

The only verbs in this group are:

bleiben	*to remain*	scheinen	*to seem*
heißen	*to be called*	sein	*to be*
nennen	*to name*	werden	*to become*
	(in passive only)		

30.6 Verbs + prepositions

Some German verbs are used in fixed expressions with a
particular preposition, which determines the case of the
following noun or pronoun (see 15.2–5).

The most common verb + preposition combinations are
listed below under the cases which they require. The
prepositions which can take either accusative or dative
(15.4) are printed in bold; for these, it is necessary to
memorize the case required by the verb + preposition
combination.

■ **30.6.1** Verbs with preposition + accusative

achten **auf**	*to pay attention to, keep an eye on*
bitten um	*to ask for*
denken **an**	*to be thinking about*
denken **über**	*to hold an opinion of, think of*
kämpfen um	*to fight for*

nachdenken **über**	to ponder, reflect on
warten **auf**	to wait for
sich amüsieren **über**	to laugh at, smile about
sich ärgern **über**	to get annoyed about/with
sich bewerben um	to apply for
sich erinnern **an**	to remember
sich freuen **über/auf**	to be pleased about/look forward to
sich gewöhnen **an**	to get used to
sich interessieren für	to be interested in
sich kümmern um	to take care of, see to
sich unterhalten **über**	to talk about
sich verlassen **auf**	to rely on, depend on

■ **30.6.2** Verbs with preposition + dative

abhängen von	to be dependent on
bestehen aus	to consist of
leiden **an/unter**	to suffer from
neigen zu	to be inclined to
riechen nach	to smell of
schmecken nach	to taste of
sterben **an**	to die of
teilnehmen **an**	to take part in
träumen von	to dream of
sich beschäftigen mit	to occupy oneself with
sich sehnen nach	to long for
sich unterhalten mit	to converse with
sich verabschieden von	to say goodbye to
sich verstehen mit	to get along with, get on with

■ **30.6.3** Verbs with preposition + genitive

anklagen wegen	to accuse of
verhaften wegen	to arrest on grounds of
verurteilen wegen	to convict of
sich schämen wegen	to be ashamed of

31 The infinitive

There are four forms of the infinitive:

	active	*passive*
present	kaufen *to buy*	gekauft werden *to be bought*
perfect	gekauft haben *to have bought*	gekauft worden sein *to have been bought*

The present active infinitive is the basic form of a verb as given in a dictionary, such as **kaufen** (*to buy*) and **machen** (*to make*), and is generally simply referred to as 'the infinitive'. It is the most widely used form and is therefore the focus of this section.

31.1 The infinitive with zu

Most infinitive constructions in German are accompanied by **zu**. The equivalent in English is often a 'to' or '-ing' form. Note that in German the infinitive is placed at the end of the phrase.

Wir haben vor, am Sonntag in Urlaub **zu fahren**.	*We are planning to go on holiday on Sunday.*
Er gibt zu, das gesagt **zu haben**.	*He admits having said that.*

These infinitive constructions are only possible if their subject is identical with the subject or object of the main clause. Otherwise a clause with **daß** is needed.

- Identical with subject:

Ich hoffe, dich bald wiederzusehen.	*I hope to see you again soon.*

- Identical with object:

Ich bitte **Sie**, in Zukunft pünktlich zu kommen.	*I would ask you to arrive on time in future.*

- Different subject: **daß** clause
  Ich hoffe, daß **er** bald kommt.   *I hope he'll come soon.*

■ 31.1.1 The position of zu

In the simple tenses (present and simple past) the word **zu** is always placed immediately before simple verbs and inseparable verbs (28.1).

Es war schön, von dir **zu** hören.   *It was nice to hear from you.*

With separable verbs **zu** is inserted after the prefix:

Du hast vergessen, Brot ein**zu**kaufen.   *You forgot to buy some bread.*

In the compound tenses **zu** is always placed immediately before the auxiliary:

Sie glaubte, das Auto hier geparkt **zu** haben.   *She thought she had parked the car here.*

Sie vermutet, abgeschleppt worden **zu** sein.   *She assumes that her car has been towed away.*

■ 31.1.2 The infinitive with zu after prepositions

- **um ... zu** (*in order to*)
  Ich werde alles machen, **um** diese Stelle **zu** bekommen.   *I'll do anything to get this job.*

- **ohne ... zu** (*without + '-ing'*)
  Er kaufte das Haus, **ohne** lange **zu** überlegen.   *He bought the house without deliberating for long.*

- **(an)statt ... zu** (*instead of + '-ing'*)
  Anstatt den Unfall **zu** melden, ist er einfach weitergefahren.   *Instead of reporting the accident, he simply drove on.*

These infinitive constructions can only be used if the subjects of the main clause and infinitive phrase are identical. Otherwise a construction with **damit, ohne daß** or **anstatt daß** is needed:

Ich habe den Urlaub gebucht, **damit** du dich etwas entspannst.	*I booked the holiday for you to relax a little.*
Sie verließ das Restaurant, **ohne daß** ich sie sah.	*She left the restaurant without me seeing her.*

31.2 The infinitive without zu

The following groups of verbs normally form infinitive constructions without **zu**.

■ **31.2.1** The six modal verbs (**dürfen, können, müssen, sollen, wollen, mögen**)

Ich **muß** heute nicht **arbeiten**.	*I don't have to work today.*
Die Waren **sollen** heute noch **versandt werden**.	*The goods are due to be dispatched today.*

■ **31.2.2** Verbs of perception such as **hören, sehen, fühlen, spüren**

Sie **hörte** das Kind **schreien**.	*She heard the child crying.*
Er **sah** sie schon von weitem **kommen**.	*He saw her coming a long way off.*

■ **31.2.3** Some verbs of motion such as **gehen, kommen, fahren**

Gehst du **einkaufen**?	*Are you going shopping?*
Ich **komme** mit **essen**.	*I'll come along to eat.*

31.2.4 lassen

Die Kinder **lassen** ihn nicht **schlafen**.	*The children don't let him sleep.*

31.3 The infinitive with or without zu

■ **31.3.1** If **helfen**, **lehren**, **lernen** are followed by the infinitive alone, **zu** is omitted:

Ich **helfe** aufräumen.	*I'll help tidy up.*
Er **lernt** schwimmen.	*He is learning to swim.*

If the verb is followed by more than just an infinitive, both uses are found, with or without **zu**:

Wir **helfen** dir, das Zimmer auf**zu**räumen.	*We'll help you to tidy up your room.*
Wir **helfen** dir das Zimmer aufräumen.	*We'll help you tidy up your room.*

■ **31.3.2** After **bleiben** followed by a verb of place there is no **zu**:

Er **blieb** einfach **sitzen**.	*He just remained seated.*
Sie **bleibt** noch ein Jahr dort **wohnen**.	*She will continue to live there for another year.*

In all other contexts **bleiben** is always used with **zu**:

Das **bleibt** ab**zu**warten.	*That remains to be seen.*
Es **bleibt** noch viel **zu** tun.	*There remains a lot to be done.*

■ **31.3.3** The verb **brauchen** is often used without **zu** in colloquial German. However, formal German still prefers the infinitive with **zu**.

Da brauchen wir erst gar nicht **anfangen**.	*It's hardly worth even starting this.*
Die Kündigung braucht nicht vor dem ersten April **zu erfolgen**.	*Notice does not have to be given until 1st April.*

31.4 The infinitive with passive sense

After certain verbs the infinitive has a passive sense, although its form is active. The most common of these verbs are **bleiben**, **sein** and **es gibt**:

Das **bleibt** abzuwarten.	*That remains to be seen.*
Mein Auto **ist** zu verkaufen.	*My car is for sale/to be sold.*
Es gibt viel zu sagen.	*There is much to be said.*

31.5 Other uses of the infinitive

■ **31.5.1** All infinitives may be used as nouns, their gender always being neuter. Most infinitival nouns express the action of the verb and equate to an English '-ing' form.

Das Laufen war sehr anstrengend.	*The jogging was very exhausting.*
Beim Lesen trinke ich gerne ein Glas Wein.	*I like to drink a glass of wine when I'm reading.*

A few infinitival nouns have additional meanings, e.g.:

das Essen	*eating, meal*
das Leben	*living, life*

■ **31.5.2** Infinitives are often used in written instructions, or on public notices giving commands (see also 33.2):

Karotten **schälen** und **würfeln**.	*Peel and dice the carrots.*
Einfahrt **freihalten**	*Keep entrance clear*

32 The present participle

The present participle and the more commonly used past participle (20.3) do not refer to any particular time. In German they are often called **Partizip** I and II.

32.1 Formation

The present participle is formed by adding **-d** to the infinitive:

kochen (*to cook, to boil*) ➜ kochen**d** (*cooking, boiling*)

Exceptions are the very rare forms **seiend** (*being*) and **tuend** (*doing*).

Separable verbs (28.3) remain as one word in the present participle:

vorbeigehen (*to pass*)   ➜ vorbeigehend (*passing*)

32.2 Use

In German the present participle is used far less than in English.

■ **32.2.1** It is usually found as an adjective or adjectival noun, when it is declined like an adjective (9.2).

Ich habe **kochendes**   *I fetched boiling water.*
Wasser geholt.
Die **Streikenden** stimmten   *The strikers did not agree.*
nicht zu.

■ **32.2.2** Note that the German present participle is NOT used

- for continuous tenses:
  I am going to the cinema.   Ich gehe ins Kino.

- after modal verbs and verbs of perception and motion:
  I like singing.   Ich singe gerne.
  We went swimming.   Wir sind schwimmen gegangen.

The imperative is the form of the verb which expresses commands, requests or instructions.

33.1 Formation

German has three principal imperative forms:

du	*familiar singular*	**Komm** her!	
ihr	*familiar plural*	**Kommt** her!	— *Come here!*
Sie	*formal sing./pl.*	**Kommen Sie** her!	

There is also a **wir** form for making suggestions:

Gehen wir! *Let's go!*

- The familiar imperative singular is identical with the stem of the verb (the part of the verb that is left when the infinitive ending **-en** or **-n** is removed), except for the variations detailed in 33.1.1.

- The familiar imperative plural adds **-t** to the verb stem.

- The **Sie** and **wir** forms are identical to the indicative, with the pronoun following (verb stem + **-en** + **Sie/wir**).

■ **33.1.1** Variations in the familiar imperative singular

a An **-e** is added

- If the verb stem ends in **-d** or **-t**, or in **-m** or **-n** preceded by a consonant other than **l** or **r**:

  Beantworte bitte die Frage! *Please answer the question.*
  Öffne bitte die Tür! *Please open the door!*

  If pronunciation permits, the **-e** is often omitted:
  Red(e) bitte etwas lauter! *Speak up, please!*

- if the infinitive ends in **-eln** or **-ern**. The additional **e** within the stem is usually dropped:
  Samm(e)le bitte das Geld ein! *Please collect the money.*

b The vowel is changed in all strong verbs which have a vowel change in the second and third persons singular of the present tense (e.g. **nehmen: du nimmst, er nimmt**):

Nimm das mit nach Hause! *Take it home!*
Lies mal vor! *Please read it aloud!*

However, the addition of an Umlaut (e.g. **fahren: du fährst, er fährt**) does not apply to the imperative:

Fahr nicht so schnell! *Don't drive so fast!*
Laß das! *Stop that!*

■ **33.1.2** All imperative forms of **sein** are irregular:

Sei
Seid — bitte ruhig! *Please be quiet!*
Seien Sie
Seien wir nicht kleinlich. *Let's not be mean.*

33.2 Alternatives to the imperative

The imperative may be replaced by

- an infinitive, e.g. in instructions and on signs:
  Einfahrt freihalten *Keep entrance clear*

- a past participle, e.g. in military language:
  Stillgestanden! *Attention!*

- an impersonal passive:
  Jetzt **wird geschlafen!** *Go to sleep!*

- future tense or present tense with future meaning:
  Sie **werden** jetzt die Firma *Go and phone Henkel now!*
  Henkel **anrufen!**

- nouns, adjectives or adverbs:
  Vorsicht! *Look out!*
  Schnell! *Quick!*
  Vorwärts! *Move!*

Tables 34.1 and 34.2 set out the conjugation of weak and strong verbs in all forms of the active voice. The most common strong and irregular weak verbs are listed in 34.3 with their principal forms. For the forms of the passive voice see 23.2.

34.1 Conjugation of weak verbs

The regular pattern for weak verbs is exemplified by the verb **holen** (*to get/to fetch*).

Infinitive:		**holen**	*to get*
Present participle:		**holend**	*getting*
Past participle:		**geholt**	*got*
Imperative:	(**du** form)	**hol!**	*get*
	(**ihr** form)	**holt!**	*get*
	(**Sie** form)	**holen Sie!**	*get*

Simple tenses	**Singular**	**Plural**
Present indicative		
I get,	1. ich hole	1. wir holen
I'm getting	2. du holst	2. ihr holt
	3. er/sie/es holt	3. sie/Sie holen

Simple past indicative		
I got,	1. ich holte	1. wir holten
I was getting	2. du holtest	2. ihr holtet
	3. er/sie/es holte	3. sie/Sie holten

Konjunktiv I Gegenwart (present subjunctive)		
I get,	1. ich hole	1. wir holen
I may get	2. du holest	2. ihr holet
	3. er/sie/es hole	3. sie/Sie holen

Konjunktiv II Gegenwart (past subjunctive, one-word form)		
I got,	1. ich holte	1. wir holten
I might get	2. du holtest	2. ihr holtet
	3. er/sie/es holte	3. sie/Sie holten

Compound tenses

	Singular	Plural
Perfect indicative		
I have got	1. ich **habe** ... **geholt**	1. wir **haben** ... **geholt**
	2. du **hast**	2. ihr **habt**
	3. er/sie/es **hat**	3. sie/Sie **haben**
Pluperfect indicative		
I had got	1. ich **hatte** ... **geholt**	1. wir **hatten** ... **geholt**
	2. du **hattest**	2. ihr **hattet**
	3. er/sie/es **hatte**	3. sie/Sie **hatten**
Future indicative		
I will get	1. ich **werde** ... **holen**	1. wir **werden** ... **holen**
	2. du **wirst**	2. ihr **werdet**
	3. er/sie/es **wird**	3. sie/Sie **werden**

Konjunktiv II Gegenwart (conditional, two-word form)

	Singular	Plural
I would get,	1. ich **würde** ... **holen**	1. wir **würden** ... **holen**
I might get	2. du **würdest**	2. ihr **würdet**
	3. er/sie/es **würde**	3. sie/Sie **würden**

Konjunktiv II Zukunft (future subjunctive)

	Singular	Plural
I may get	1. ich **werde** ... **holen**	1. wir **werden** ... **holen**
	2. du **werdest**	2. ihr **werdet**
	3. er/sie/es **werde**	3. sie/Sie **werden**

Konjunktiv I Vergangenheit (perfect subjunctive)

	Singular	Plural
I have got,	1. ich **habe** ... **geholt**	1. wir **haben** ... **geholt**
I may have	2. du **habest**	2. ihr **habet**
got	3. er/sie/es **habe**	3. sie/Sie **haben**

Konjunktiv II Vergangenheit (pluperfect subjunctive)

	Singular	Plural
I would/	1. ich **hätte** ... **geholt**	1. wir **hätten** ... **geholt**
might have	2. du **hättest**	2. ihr **hättet**
got	3. er/sie/es **hätte**	3. sie/Sie **hätten**

34.2 Conjugation of strong verbs

The stem vowel and consonant changes in strong verbs do not all follow the same pattern and have to be learnt individually (see list in 34.3).

The conjugation of strong verbs is exemplified by the verb **sehen** (*to see*). Like many strong verbs, it has a vowel change in the present and past tenses. The English equivalent is also a strong verb.

Infinitive:		**sehen**	*to see*
Present participle:		**sehend**	*seeing*
Past participle:		**gesehen**	*seen*
Imperative:	(**du** form)	**sieh!**	*see*
	(**ihr** form)	**seht!**	*see*
	(**Sie** form)	**sehen Sie!**	*see*

Simple tenses	**Singular**	**Plural**
Present indicative		
I see,	1. ich sehe	1. wir sehen
I'm seeing	2. du siehst	2. ihr seht
	3. er/sie/es sieht	3. sie/Sie sehen
Simple past indicative		
I saw, I was	1. ich sah	1. wir sahen
seeing	2. du sahst	2. ihr saht
	3. er/sie/es sah	3. sie/Sie sahen
Konjunktiv I Gegenwart (present subjunctive)		
I see, I may	1. ich sehe	1. wir sehen
see	2. du sehest	2. ihr sehet
	3. er/sie/es sehe	3. sie/Sie sehen
Konjunktiv II Gegenwart (past subjunctive, one-word form)		
I saw, I might	1. ich sähe	1. wir sähen
see	2. du sähest	2. ihr sähet
	3. er/sie/es sähe	3. sie/Sie sähen

Compound tenses

	Singular	Plural
Perfect indicative		
I have seen	1. ich **habe ... gesehen**	1. wir **haben ... gesehen**
	2. du **hast**	2. ihr **habt**
	3. er/sie/es **hat**	3. sie/Sie **haben**
Pluperfect indicative		
I had seen	1. ich **hatte ... gesehen**	1. wir **hatten ... gesehen**
	2. du **hattest**	2. ihr **hattet**
	3. er/sie/es **hatte**	3. sie/Sie **hatten**
Future indicative		
I will see	1. ich **werde ... sehen**	1. wir **werden ... sehen**
	2. du **wirst**	2. ihr **werdet**
	3. er/sie/es **wird**	3. sie/Sie **werden**

Konjunktiv II Gegenwart (conditional, two-word form)

I would see,	1. ich **würde ... sehen**	1. wir **würden ... sehen**
I might see	2. du **würdest**	2. ihr **würdet**
	3. er/sie/es **würde**	3. sie/Sie **würden**

Konjunktiv II Zukunft (future indicative)

I may see	1. ich **werde ... sehen**	1. wir **werden ... sehen**
	2. du **werdest**	2. ihr **werdet**
	3. er/sie/es **werde**	3. sie/Sie **werden**

Konjunktiv I Vergangenheit (perfect subjunctive)

I have seen,	1. ich **habe ... gesehen**	1. wir **haben ... gesehen**
I may have	2. du **habest**	2. ihr **habet**
seen	3. er/sie/es **habe**	3. sie/Sie **haben**

Konjunktiv II Vergangenheit (pluperfect subjunctive)

I would/	1. ich **hätte ... gesehen**	1. wir **hätten ... gesehen**
might have	2. du **hättest**	2. ihr **hättet**
seen	3. er/sie/es **hätte**	3. sie/Sie **hätten**

34.3 List of strong and irregular verbs

The following list gives the principal forms of the most commonly used strong and irregular weak (or 'mixed') verbs. With few exceptions, compound verbs formed from these verbs follow the same pattern as the base verb.

The third person singular is given for each tense. Where the **Konjunktiv II Gegenwart** (one-word) forms are different from the simple past, they are given in brackets. **Haben, sein, werden** (25.3) and the modal verbs (26.2.1) have further irregularities in the present tense.

Infinitive	Present	Simple past (+ Konjunktiv II)	Past participle + **haben/sein**	*Basic meaning*
backen	backt	backte	hat gebacken	*to bake*
befehlen	befiehlt	befahl (beföhle)	hat befohlen	*to command*
beginnen	beginnt	begann (begänne)	hat begonnen	*to begin*
beißen	beißt	biß (bisse)	hat gebissen	*to bite*
bergen	birgt	barg (bärge)	hat geborgen	*to rescue/ to hide*
bersten	birst	barst (bärste)	ist geborsten	*to burst*
betrügen	betrügt	betrog (betröge)	hat betrogen	*to deceive*
biegen	biegt	bog (böge)	hat/ist gebogen	*to bend/ to turn*
bieten	bietet	bot (böte)	hat geboten	*to offer*
binden	bindet	band (bände)	hat gebunden	*to tie*
bitten	bittet	bat (bäte)	hat gebeten	*to request*
blasen	bläst	blies (bliese)	hat geblasen	*to blow*
bleiben	bleibt	blieb (bliebe)	ist geblieben	*to remain*
braten	brät	briet (briete)	hat gebraten	*to fry/to roast*
brechen	bricht	brach (bräche)	hat/ist gebrochen	*to break*
brennen	brennt	brannte (brennte)	hat gebrannt	*to burn*
bringen	bringt	brachte (brächte)	hat gebracht	*to bring*
denken	denkt	dachte (dächte)	hat gedacht	*to think*
dringen	dringt	drang (dränge)	hat/ist gedrungen	*to penetrate*

dürfen	darf	durfte (dürfte)	hat gedurft/ dürfen	to be allowed to
empfehlen	empfiehlt	empfahl (empföhle)	hat empfohlen	to recommend
erlöschen	erlischt	erlosch (erlösche)	ist erloschen	to go out (of fire)
erschrecken (intransitive)	erschrickt	erschrak (erschräke)	ist erschrocken	to be startled
erwägen	erwägt	erwog (erwöge)	hat erwogen	to weigh up
essen	ißt	aß (äße)	hat gegessen	to eat
fahren	fährt	fuhr (führe)	hat/ist gefahren	to travel/ to drive
fallen	fällt	fiel (fiele)	ist gefallen	to fall
fangen	fängt	fing (finge)	hat gefangen	to catch
finden	findet	fand (fände)	hat gefunden	to find
fliegen	fliegt	flog (flöge)	hat/ist geflogen	to fly
fliehen	flieht	floh (flöhe)	hat/ist geflohen	to escape
fließen	fließt	floß (flösse)	ist geflossen	to flow
fressen	frißt	fraß (fräße)	hat gefressen	to eat (of animals)
gebären	gebiert	gebar (gebäre)	hat geboren	to give birth to
geben	gibt	gab (gäbe)	hat gegeben	to give
gehen	geht	ging (ginge)	ist gegangen	to go
gelingen	gelingt	gelang (gelänge)	ist gelungen	to succeed
gelten	gilt	galt (gälte)	hat gegolten	to be valid
genießen	genießt	genoß (genösse)	hat genossen	to enjoy
geraten	gerät	geriet (geriete)	ist geraten	to get into
geschehen	geschieht	geschah (geschähe)	ist geschehen	to happen
gewinnen	gewinnt	gewann (gewänne/gewönne)	hat gewonnen	to win
gießen	gießt	goß (gösse)	hat gegossen	to pour
gleichen	gleicht	glich (gliche)	hat geglichen	to resemble
gleiten	gleitet	glitt (glitte)	ist geglitten	to glide
graben	gräbt	grub (grübe)	hat gegraben	to dig
greifen	greift	griff (griffe)	hat gegriffen	to grip
haben	hat	hatte (hätte)	hat gehabt	to have

halten	hält	hielt (hielte)	hat gehalten	to hold
hängen (intransitive)	hängt	hing (hinge)	hat gehangen	to hang
heben	hebt	hob (höbe)	hat gehoben	to lift
heißen	heißt	hieß (hieße)	hat geheißen	to be called
helfen	hilft	half (hülfe/hälfe)	hat geholfen	to help
kennen	kennt	kannte (kennte)	hat gekannt	to know
klingen	klingt	klang (klänge)	hat geklungen	to sound
kommen	kommt	kam (kame)	ist gekommen	to come
können	kann	konnte (könnte)	hat gekonnt/können	to be able to
kriechen	kriecht	kroch (kröche)	ist gekrochen	to crawl
laden	lädt	lud (lüde)	hat geladen	to load
lassen	läßt	ließ (ließe)	hat gelassen	to allow
laufen	läuft	lief (liefe)	hat/ist gelaufen	to run
leiden	leidet	litt (litte)	hat gelitten	to suffer
leihen	leiht	lieh (liehe)	hat geliehen	to lend/to borrow
lesen	liest	las (läse)	hat gelesen	to read
liegen	liegt	lag (läge)	hat/ist gelegen	to lie
lügen	lügt	log (löge)	hat gelogen	to tell a lie
meiden	meidet	mied (miede)	hat gemieden	to avoid
messen	mißt	maß (mäße)	hat gemessen	to measure
mißlingen	mißlingt	mißlang (mißlänge)	ist mißlungen	to fail
mögen	mag	mochte (möchte)	hat gemocht/mögen	to like
müssen	muß	mußte (müßte)	hat gemußt/müssen	to have to
nehmen	nimmt	nahm (nähme)	hat genommen	to take
nennen	nennt	nannte (nennte)	hat genannt	to name
pfeifen	pfeift	pfiff (pfiffe)	hat gepfiffen	to call
raten	rät	riet (riete)	hat geraten	to advise
reiben	reibt	rieb (riebe)	hat gerieben	to rub
reißen	reißt	riß (risse)	hat/ist gerissen	to tear
reiten	reitet	ritt (ritte)	hat/ist geritten	to ride
rennen	rennt	rannte (rennte)	hat/ist gerannt	to run
riechen	riecht	roch (röche)	hat gerochen	to smell

rufen	ruft	rief (riefe)	hat gerufen	*to shout*
saufen	säuft	soff (söffe)	hat gesoffen	*to swill*
schaffen	schafft	schuf (schüfe)	hat geschaffen	*to create*
scheiden	scheidet	schied (schiede)	hat/ist geschieden	*to separate*
scheinen	scheint	schien (schiene)	hat geschienen	*to shine*
schieben	schiebt	schob (schöbe)	hat geschoben	*to shove*
schießen	schießt	schoß (schösse)	hat/ist geschossen	*to shoot*
schlafen	schläft	schlief (schliefe)	hat geschlafen	*to sleep*
schlagen	schlägt	schlug (schlüge)	hat geschlagen	*to hit*
schleichen	schleicht	schlich (schliche)	ist geschlichen	*to creep*
schließen	schließt	schloß (schlösse)	hat geschlossen	*to close*
schmeißen	schmeißt	schmiß (schmisse)	hat geschmissen	*to fling*
schmelzen	schmilzt	schmolz (schmölze)	hat/ist geschmolzen	*to melt*
schneiden	schneidet	schnitt (schnitte)	hat geschnitten	*to cut*
schreiben	schreibt	schrieb (schriebe)	hat geschrieben	*to write*
schreien	schreit	schrie (schriee)	hat geschrie(e)n	*to shout*
schreiten	schreitet	schritt (schritte)	ist geschritten	*to stride*
schweigen	schweigt	schwieg (schwiege)	hat geschwiegen	*to be silent*
schwimmen	schwimmt	schwamm (schwömme/schwämme)	hat/ist geschwommen	*to swim*
schwingen	schwingt	schwang (schwänge)	hat geschwungen	*to swing*
schwören	schwört	schwor (schwüre)	hat geschworen	*to vow*
sehen	sieht	sah (sähe)	hat gesehen	*to see*
sein	ist	war (wäre)	ist gewesen	*to be*
senden	sendet	sandte/sendete* (sendete)	hat gesandt/gesendet*	*to send, *to broadcast*
singen	singt	sang (sänge)	hat gesungen	*to sing*
sinken	sinkt	sank (sänke)	ist gesunken	*to sink*
sitzen	sitzt	saß (säße)	hat gesessen	*to sit*
sollen	soll	sollte	hat gesollt/sollen	*to be supposed to*
spinnen	spinnt	spann (spänne/spönne)	hat gesponnen	*to spin*

sprechen	spricht	sprach (spräche)	hat gesprochen	to speak
springen	springt	sprang (spränge)	ist gesprungen	to jump
stehen	steht	stand (stünde/stände)	hat gestanden	to stand
stehlen	stiehlt	stahl (stähle)	hat gestohlen	to steal
steigen	steigt	stieg (stiege)	ist gestiegen	to climb
sterben	stirbt	starb (stürbe)	ist gestorben	to die
stinken	stinkt	stank (stänke)	hat gestunken	to stink
stoßen	stößt	stieß (stieße)	hat/ist gestoßen	to knock/ to push
streiten	streitet	stritt (stritte)	hat gestritten	to quarrel
tragen	trägt	trug (trüge)	hat getragen	to carry/to wear
treffen	trifft	traf (träfe)	hat getroffen	to meet
treiben	treibt	trieb (triebe)	hat/ist getrieben	to drive
treten	tritt	trat (träte)	hat/ist getreten	to step
trinken	trinkt	trank (tränke)	hat getrunken	to drink
tun	tut	tat (täte)	hat getan	to do
verderben	verdirbt	verdarb (verdürbe)	hat/ist verdorben	to spoil
vergessen	vergißt	vergaß (vergäße)	hat vergessen	to forget
verlieren	verliert	verlor (verlöre)	hat verloren	to lose
wachsen	wächst	wuchs (wüchse)	ist gewachsen	to grow
waschen	wäscht	wusch (wüsche)	hat gewaschen	to wash
weisen	weist	wies (wiese)	hat gewiesen	to point
wenden	wendet	wandte/ wendete*(wendete)	hat gewandt/ gewendet*	to turn *e.g. car
werben	wirbt	warb (würbe)	hat geworben	to recruit
werden	wird	wurde (würde)	ist geworden/ worden	to become
werfen	wirft	warf (würfe)	hat geworfen	to throw
wiegen	wiegt	wog (wöge)	hat gewogen	to weigh
winden	windet	wand (wände)	hat gewunden	to wind
wissen	weiß	wußte (wüßte)	hat gewußt	to know
wollen	will	wollte	hat gewollt/ wollen	to want
ziehen	zieht	zog (zöge)	hat/ist gezogen	to pull
zwingen	zwingt	zwang (zwänge)	hat gezwungen	to force

35 Conjunctions

Conjunctions are used to link single words, phrases or clauses. It is necessary to distinguish between co-ordinating conjunctions (35.1), subordinating conjunctions (35.2) and conjunctions used with inversion (35.3), because each type of conjunction has a different effect on the word order of the sentence.

35.1 Co-ordinating conjunctions

Co-ordinating conjunctions link single words, phrases or clauses of equal status. They do not affect the word order of the clause they introduce. There are two categories of co-ordinating conjunctions: simple or one-word conjunctions (e.g. **und**, *and*) and double conjunctions (e.g. **sowohl ... als (auch)**, *both ... and*).

■ **35.1.1** The most common simple co-ordinating conjunctions are:

aber *but, however*	sondern *but, on the contrary*
denn *for*	und *and*
oder *or*	

Other simple co-ordinating conjunctions are **beziehungsweise** (*or*), **jedoch** (*but*) and **sowie** (*as well as*).

* **aber** (*but, however*)
  Beate ist noch nicht hier, *Beate hasn't arrived yet but*
  aber sie kommt gleich. *she'll be here soon.*

  Where **aber** translates as *however* it is frequently placed after the subject or the verb:
  Die Angestellten gingen *The employees went home.*
  nach Hause, der Chef **aber** *However, the boss had to*
  mußte (*or:* mußte **aber**) *continue working for*
  noch eine Stunde länger *another hour.*
  arbeiten.

- **denn** (*for, because*)

  Sie war traurig, **denn** niemand hatte sie eingeladen.

  She was sad, for/because nobody had invited her

- **oder** (*or*)

  Möchtest du Tee **oder** Kaffee?

  Would you like tea or coffee?

  Laß den Hund in Ruhe, **oder** er beißt dich noch.

  Leave the dog alone or he'll bite you.

- **sondern** (*but, on the contrary*) after negative statements

  Wir hatten uns nicht für heute, **sondern** für morgen verabredet.

  We didn't arrange to meet today, but tomorrow.

  Er war überhaupt nicht krank, **sondern** sehr gesund.

  He wasn't ill at all, on the contrary he was very well.

- **und** (*and*)

  Sie möchte einen neuen Fernseher, **und** er will ein neues Auto.

  She would like a new TV and he wants a new car.

■ **35.1.2** Common double co-ordinating conjunctions are:

entweder ... oder	*either ... or*
nicht nur ... sondern auch	*not only ... but also*
sowohl ... als (auch)	*both ... and*
weder ... noch	*neither ... nor*

- **entweder ... oder** (*either ... or*)

  Wir fahren **entweder** in die Schweiz **oder** nach Österreich.

  We go either to Switzerland or to Austria.

  When **entweder** is placed first, subject and verb normally change position (inversion), but normal word order is maintained after **oder**:

Entweder fahren wir in die Schweiz **oder** (wir fahren) nach Österreich.

Normal word order may be used after **entweder** for emphasis.

- **nicht nur** ... **sondern auch** (*not only ... but also*)

Die Autos sind **nicht nur** teuer **sondern auch** sehr laut.	*The cars are not only expensive but also very noisy.*

For emphasis, **nicht nur** can be placed at the beginning of the sentence and is then followed by inversion:

Nicht nur teuer sind sie **sondern auch** sehr laut.	*Not only are they expensive but also very noisy.*

If **sondern auch** is used to introduce another clause, the two words are usually separated:

Er kommt **nicht nur** täglich zu spät, **sondern** er geht **auch** früher.	*Not only is he late every day but he also leaves earlier.*

- **sowohl** ... **als/wie** (**auch**) (*both ... and*)
The verb is usually placed after **als** (**auch**) and has a plural ending, whether the subjects are singular or plural:

Sowohl meine Frau **als** (**auch**) meine Tochter haben sich über Ihren Besuch gefreut.	*Both my wife and my daughter enjoyed your visit.*

- **weder** ... **noch** (*neither ... nor*)

Susan spricht **weder** Deutsch **noch** Französisch.	*Susan speaks neither French nor German.*

35.2 Subordinating conjunctions

A subordinate clause cannot stand on its own, but amplifies the meaning of the main clause. Subordinating conjunctions link subordinate clauses with main clauses. They are placed at the beginning of the subordinate clause, with the verb at the end.

■ **35.2.1** **Daß** (*that*) is principally used to introduce indirect statements.

Sie sagte, **daß** er nicht zu Hause sei. — *She said that he wasn't at home.*

In everyday language **daß** is often omitted, especially before a subjunctive, in which case normal word order is used:

Sie sagte, er sei nicht zu Hause. — *She said that he wasn't at home.*

However, **daß** must be used if the statement in the main clause is negative:

Der Arzt glaubt nicht, **daß** das Bein gebrochen ist. — *The doctor doesn't think that the leg is broken.*

■ **35.2.2** **Ob** (*whether, if*) introduces indirect questions expecting a 'yes/no' answer.

Weißt du, **ob** sie da ist? — *Do you know if she is in?*

■ **35.2.3** Conjunctions introducing reasons are also called causal conjunctions. The most common of these are:

da *as, since*   weil *because*
nun da/wo *seeing that*   zumal *especially as*

- **da** (*as, since*), **weil** (*because*)
  Whereas the more emphatic **weil** usually follows the main clause, **da** tends to precede it:
  Ich konnte nicht Tennis spielen, **weil** ich verletzt war. — *I couldn't play tennis because I was injured.*

Da heute mein Geburtstag *Since it's my birthday today,*
ist, trinken wir *we'll drink champagne.*
Champagner.

- **nun da/wo** (*seeing that*)
  Nun da alles fertig ist, *Now that everything is ready*
  können die Gäste kommen. *the guests can come.*

  Nun wo and **wo** are more colloquial alternatives.

■ **35.2.4** Common conjunctions introducing conditions
(conditional conjunctions) are:

es sei denn, daß *unless*	vorausgesetzt, daß *provided that*
falls *if, in case*	wenn *if*

- **wenn** (*if*), **falls** (*if, in case*)
  Wenn is by far the most common conditional
  conjunction, but it is often replaced by **falls** to avoid
  confusion with **wenn** (*when*) (35.2.5).
  Wenn ich nichts von Ihnen *If I don't hear from you,*
  höre, bin ich um 20 Uhr da. *I'll be there at 8 p.m.*
  Ruf mich bitte an, **falls** *Please call me if something*
  etwas schiefgeht. *goes wrong.*

- **es sei denn, daß** (*unless*)
  Sie kommt um ein Uhr, **es** *She'll arrive at one o'clock,*
  sei denn, daß der Bus *unless the bus is late.*
  Verspätung hat.

  The **daß** is often omitted, in which case the following
  conditional clause has normal word order:
  Sie kommt um ein Uhr, **es sei denn**, der Bus hat Verspätung.

■ **35.2.5** Common conjunctions indicating time are:

als *when*	seitdem/seit *since*	wann *when*
bis *until*	während *while*	wenn *when*
nachdem *after*		

Other time conjunctions are **bevor** (*before*), **sobald** (*as soon as*), **solange** (*as long as*) and **sooft** (*as often as*).

- **als**, **wenn** and **wann** are all used for English *when*. While **als** refers to a single event in the past, **wenn** is used for present and future events and for repeated actions in the past (*whenever*) (see also 35.2.4):

Als sie schließlich kam, mußten wir gehen.	*When she finally arrived we had to go.*
Wenn es regnet, tapezieren wir die Wohnung.	*When it rains we'll decorate the flat.*
Es regnete immer, **wenn** wir Fußball spielen wollten.	*It always rained when(ever) we wanted to play football.*

  Wann is used for indirect questions:

Wir wissen nicht, **wann** der Elektriker kommt.	*We don't know when the electrician is coming.*

- **bis** (*until, by the time that*)

Wir müssen warten, **bis** die Lieferung ankommt.	*We have to wait until the delivery arrives.*
Bis sie die Postkarte erhält, bist du wieder zu Hause.	*You'll be back by the time she receives the postcard.*

  The negative of **bis** is **erst als** or **erst wenn** (*not until*):

Ich konnte **erst** aus dem Haus, **als** der Babysitter kam.	*I couldn't leave the house until the babysitter came.*

- **nachdem** (*after*)

Nachdem wir angekommen waren, ruhten wir uns aus.	*After we had arrived we took a rest.*

- **seitdem**, **seit** (*since*)
  Especially in informal language, **seitdem** is often replaced by the shorter **seit**.

Seitdem/Seit du allein lebst, bist du selbständiger geworden.

Since you've been living on your own, you've become more independent.

- **während** (*while, whilst*)

  Während er einkaufen war, habe ich das Essen gemacht.

  While he was shopping I prepared the meal.

  Sie ist sehr freundlich, **während** er mehr reserviert ist.

  She is very friendly whilst he is more reserved.

■ **35.2.6** Common conjunctions indicating place are:

wo *where* wohin *where (to)*
woher *where from*

They are used in relative clauses and indirect questions:

Das ist ein Ort, **wo** ich gerne leben möchte.

That's a place where I would like to live.

Er hat mir nicht gesagt, **woher** er kam.

He didn't tell me where he came from.

Bitte sag mir, **wohin** du gehst.

Please tell me where you are going.

■ **35.2.7** Common conjunctions indicating manner or degree are:

als *than* indem *by + '-ing'*
als ob *as if, as though* soweit *as far as*
dadurch, daß *by + '-ing'* wie *as*

- **als** (*than*), **wie** (*as, like*) in comparative clauses

  Die Gäste sind früher gegangen, **als** wir erwartet hatten.

  The guests left earlier than we had expected.

  Das Essen war nicht so gut, **wie** wir gedacht hatten.

  The meal was not as good as we had thought.

- **als ob** (*as if, as though*) in hypothetical comparisons
  Er tat so, **als ob** er der   *He acted as if he were the boss.*
  Chef wäre.

  The **ob** is often omitted, in which case normal word
  order is used:
  Er tat so, **als** wäre er der Chef.

- **dadurch, daß** or **indem** (*by + '-ing'*)
  Er bestand die Examen   *He passed his exams only by*
  nur, **indem (dadurch, daß)** *copying from other people.*
  er von anderen abschrieb.

■ **35.2.8** Common conjunctions stating a purpose or
result are **damit** and **so daß**:

- **damit** (*so that*) states a purpose:
  Sie arbeitet an der   *She works at the petrol station*
  Tankstelle, **damit** sie sich *so that they can afford a new*
  ein neues Auto leisten   *car.*
  können.

- **so daß** (*so that*) states a result:
  Es wurde schon dunkel, **so** *It was already getting dark,*
  daß man kaum etwas   *so (that) you could hardly*
  sehen konnte.   *see anything.*

  The **so** may also be placed in front of an adjective or
  adverb in the main clause:
  Der Umzug war **so** teuer,   *The move was so expensive*
  daß wir uns keine neuen   *that we couldn't afford*
  Möbel leisten konnten.   *new furniture.*

■ **35.2.9** The main conjunctions stating an opposing
reason (concessive conjunctions) are:
  obwohl *although*   zwar ... aber *although*
  so/wie ... auch *however*

- **obwohl** (*although*) is the most common of these.

  Ich bin Tennis spielen | *I went to play tennis*
  gegangen, **obwohl** ich | *although I was very*
  sehr müde war. | *tired.*

  An everyday alternative to **obwohl** is **zwar ... aber** (*although*):

  Sie ist **zwar** sehr beliebt, | *Although she's very popular,*
  aber (sie ist) nicht sehr | *she's not very intelligent.*
  intelligent.

- **so/wie ... auch** (*however*)

  So/Wie schnell du **auch** | *However fast you drive, you*
  fährst, du kommst nicht | *won't arrive on time.*
  mehr rechtzeitig an.

  As in English, the same construction can be used with interrogative pronouns, e.g. **wann ... auch** (*whenever*), **was für ... auch** (*whatever*), **wer ... auch** (*whoever*).

35.3 Conjunctions used with inversion

Some adverbs are frequently used to link clauses and are therefore called adverbial conjunctions. When placed at the beginning of a clause, they are usually followed by inversion of subject and verb (36.1.2). Conjunctions in this group include:

allerdings	*admittedly, to be sure*
dagegen	*on the other hand*
deshalb	*therefore*
freilich	*admittedly, to be sure*
sonst	*otherwise*
trotzdem	*nevertheless, anyway*

Der Urlaub war insgesamt | *The holiday was in general*
sehr schön, **allerdings/** | *very good. Admittedly it rained*
freilich hat es viel | *a lot.*
geregnet.

Word order

Word order in German can be much more flexible
than in English, because subjects and objects are
differentiated by case endings; the word order can
therefore be varied for reasons of emphasis. However,
there is a 'standard', unemphatic order for main clause
statements (36.1), questions and commands (36.2) and
subordinate clauses (36.3). The position of **nicht** is
treated in 13.1.

36.1 Main clause statements

■ **36.1.1** Subject and verb: standard order

In main clauses the subject is normally the first element.
The second element is almost always the conjugated verb
(verb 1). In the case of verbs with more than one part, the
non-conjugated part (verb 2) is placed at the end of the
clause. Thus the verb provides a kind of 'bracket' dividing
a sentence into three different parts: an initial position
before the first bracket (**Vorfeld**), a main part inside the
bracket (**Mittelfeld**) and a final position after the second
bracket (**Nachfeld**).

Vorfeld	Verb 1	Mittelfeld	Verb 2	Nachfeld
Sie	**kam**	gestern um ein Uhr.		
Ich	**möchte**	nicht ins Kino	**gehen**.	
Ich	**habe**	ihm 20 Mark	**gegeben**,	weil ...
Ihr	**seid**	viel schneller	**gefahren**	als wir.
Sie	**ist**	mittags ins Café	**gegangen**	und nicht ins Büro.

(*She came yesterday at one o'clock. I don't want to go to the
cinema. I gave him 20 marks, because ... You drove much faster
than we did. She went to the café at lunchtime and not to the
office.*)

Anything preceding the first element, such as interjections, **ja/nein** and names of persons addressed, is regarded as standing outside the clause and is usually separated from it by a comma:

Ach, ich fühle mich nicht gut.	*Oh, I don't feel well.*
Nein, wir machen das nicht.	*No, we won't do that.*
Beate, ich komme mit.	*Beate, I'm coming with you.*

A co-ordinating conjunction (35.1) also precedes the first element and does not affect the word order:

Sie ist nett, **aber** sie kann keinen Spaß vertragen.	*She is nice but she can't take a joke.*

■ **36.1.2** Subject and verb: inversion for emphasis
Although the subject is usually placed in the initial position (**Vorfeld**), another word, a phrase or a subordinate clause may be placed here, often to give it emphasis. The positions of subject and verb are then inverted:

Jetzt hole ich einen Kaffee.	*Now I'll get a coffee.*
In München ist die Maschine gerade gelandet.	*The plane has just landed in Munich.*

■ **36.1.3** Special verbs

a In verb combinations of more than two parts (e.g. a double infinitive or a compound passive tense) the non-conjugated part of the auxiliary verb (verb 3) is placed at the end of the clause:

Vorfeld	Verb 1	Mittelfeld	Verb 2	Verb 3
Wir	**hätten**	das Auto	**verkaufen**	**sollen**.
Ich	**werde**	dies noch	**erledigen**	**müssen**.
Sie	**ist**	von ihrem Freund	**abgeholt**	**worden**.

(*We should have sold the car. I'll still have to do that. She was picked up by her boyfriend.*)

b When separable verbs (28.3) are used in the simple tenses, the prefix is placed at the end of the clause:

Sie **ruft** ihn **an**.   *She's going to phone him.*

In compound tenses or with a modal auxiliary, the prefix remains joined to the separable verb at the end of the clause:

Er hat das Licht **ausgemacht**.   *He switched off the light.*
Ich möchte **ausgehen**.   *I'd like to go out.*

c The reflexive pronoun (27.2) usually immediately follows the conjugated verb:

Wir **verabschieden uns** jetzt.   *We are going to say goodbye now.*
Ich **habe mich** gestern erkältet.   *I caught a cold yesterday.*

However, if there is inversion (36.1.2) and if the subject is a pronoun, the verb and reflexive pronoun are separated by it:

Jetzt **verabschieden** wir **uns**.
Gestern **habe** ich **mich** erkältet.

But:

Gestern **hat sich** Peter erkältet.

■ **36.1.4** Objects and other elements
Most elements in a sentence are placed inside the bracket formed by the different parts of the verb (**Mittelfeld**). The **Nachfeld** remains for subordinate clauses, comparative phrases and occasionally for other elements if these are stressed.

a Objects may be nouns, pronouns or phrases. As in English, the indirect object (8.1.3) normally precedes the direct object (8.1.2):

Sie hat **ihm** *(dat.)* **einen Ring** *(acc.)* geschenkt.   *She gave him a ring.*

Wir bieten **unseren Kunden** *We offer our customers an*
einen exzellenten Service. *excellent service.*

However, if the direct object is a personal pronoun
(**ihn/sie/es**), it precedes the indirect object.

Uwe holt **ihn** *(acc.)* **dir**   *Uwe will fetch him for you.*
(dat.). Claudia leiht **es**   *Claudia will lend it to her*
(acc.) **ihrer** Schwester *(dat.)*. *sister.*

To emphasize them, objects can be placed in the **Vorfeld**.
English uses different constructions to achieve this:

Dieses Haus würde ich   *This is the house I'd like*
gerne kaufen.   *to buy.*
Meinem Bruder wurde   *My brother had his new car*
das neue Auto gestohlen.   *stolen.*

b Elements other than the subject and the direct or
indirect object are usually placed at the end of the
Mittelfeld. These include:

• adverbs/expressions of place and direction
Gestern bin ich **im Büro**   *I was in the office yesterday.*
gewesen.
Wir werden nächstes Jahr   *We are flying to Acapulco*
nach Acapulco fliegen.   *next year.*

• complements of the verbs **sein**, **werden**, etc. (30.5)
Er ist bis letztes Jahr **ein**   *Until last year he was a*
sehr reicher Mann   *very rich man.*
gewesen.

• prepositional phrases
Sie hat lange **auf den Bus**   *She waited a long time for*
gewartet.   *the bus.*

• genitive objects
Er wurde **des Mordes**   *He was accused of murder.*
angeklagt.

However, to emphasize them, any of these elements may be placed in the **Vorfeld** or, in colloquial speech, in the **Nachfeld**:

> **Nach Acapulco** werden wir nächstes Jahr fliegen.
> **Auf den Bus** hat sie lange gewartet.
> Wir werden das machen,   *We'll do that before our*
> **vor unserem Urlaub.**   *holiday.*

■ 36.1.5 Adverbs
The standard order of adverbs and adverbial phrases is:

	time	manner	place	
Wir haben	**gestern**	viel	**im Garten**	gespielt.
Du hast	**lange**	bequem	**auf dem Sofa**	geschlafen.
Er fährt	**morgen**	mit mir	**nach Hamburg.**	

(We played a lot in the garden yesterday. You slept comfortably on the sofa for a long time. He'll go to Hamburg with me tomorrow.)

The position of adverbs in the clause is extremely flexible, but the following are guidelines.

- Adverbs follow pronoun objects:
  Sie hat es mir **gestern**   *She gave it to me yesterday.*
  gegeben.

- Most are placed before an accusative noun object:
  Man wird Ihnen **bei der**   *They'll give you a voucher*
  Kasse einen Gutschein   *at the checkout.*
  geben.

- However, adverbs of manner tend to follow the accusative object:
  Sie schickte Ihnen das   *She sent you the document*
  Dokument **per Post.**   *by post.*

- Unemphatic adverbs of other categories may precede even the dative noun object:

| Sie hat **heute** dem Nachbarn den Rasen gemäht. | *She cut her neighbour's lawn today.* |

For emphasis, adverbs are often placed in the **Vorfeld** or at the end of the **Mittelfeld**:

| **Letzte Woche** hat er dem Kunden den Kühlschrank repariert. | *It was last week that he repaired the customer's fridge.* |
| Er hat dem Kunden den Kühlschrank **letzte Woche** repariert. | |

36.2 Questions and commands

In questions expecting the answer 'yes/no' and in commands, the conjugated verb is normally the first element. The subject (if any) is placed second. As in main clause statements, other parts of the verb are placed at the end:

Verb 1	Other elements	Verb 2
Fahren	Sie in die Stadt?	
Könnten	Sie mir das Salz	**reichen**?
Hilf	ihm bitte!	

(*Are you going into town? Could you pass me the salt? Please help him.*)

However, in questions with an interrogative word or phrase this precedes the verb. The subject then follows the verb:

Interrogative	Verb 1	Other elements
Was	**machst**	du?
Welches Eis	**möchtet**	ihr?

(*What are you doing? Which ice cream would you like?*)

The position of all other elements is as in statements, explained in 36.1.3–5.

36.3 Subordinate clauses

■ 36.3.1 Normal order

The subordinating conjunction (35.2) is placed at the beginning of the subordinate clause. The conjugated verb is usually placed at the end, and other parts of the verb immediately precede it.

Conjunction	Other elements	Verb 2	Verb 1
Als	sie		**kam**, ...
Weil	er nicht	**gehen**	**konnte**, ...
Obwohl	ich ihn	**gerufen**	**hatte**, ...

(When she arrived ..., Because he couldn't walk ..., Although I had called him ...)

However, if there are two or more infinitives at the end, the conjugated verb precedes these:

> Obwohl ich immer **habe**   *Although I always had to*
> arbeiten müssen, ...   *work ...*

If the same verb applies to two or more consecutive subordinate clauses, it is placed at the end of the last clause:

> Sie kann nicht kommen,   *She can't come because*
> weil sie arbeiten (muß)   *she has to work and*
> und sich auf das Examen   *prepare for the exam.*
> vorbereiten **muß**.

■ 36.3.2 Special verbs

a Separable verbs are united with their prefix at the end of the clause:

> Ich komme, wenn du mich   *I'll come if you pick me up.*
> **abholst**.

b With reflexive verbs, the reflexive pronoun follows a pronoun subject but may precede or follow a noun subject:

Als er **sich** rasierte, ...   *When he shaved ...*

Als Karl **sich** rasierte, ... ⎤
                   ├ *When Karl shaved ...*
Als **sich** Karl rasierte, ... ⎦

c Separable reflexive verbs follow both the rules above:

Während du **dich**   *While you are changing, ...*
umziehst, ...

Während **sich** Marion   *While Marion is changing, ...*
umzieht, ...

■ 36.3.3 Other elements

The position of other elements in the clause is the same as in main clauses (36.1.3–5), except that they are always placed between the subject and the verb.

■ 36.3.4 Exceptions

a Indirect speech clauses without the conjunction **daß** follow the pattern of main clause statements (36.1):

Sie sagte, sie **sei** einsam.   *She said she was lonely.*

Er meint, sie **kommen**   *He reckons they'll come at*
um 14.00 Uhr.   *2 p.m.*

b Conditional clauses (35.2.4) without conjunctions and hypothetical comparative clauses with **als**, where **ob** is omitted, follow the inversion pattern of questions and commands (36.2):

Hätten wir mehr Geld, so *If we had more money we*
würden wir ein Haus   *would buy a house.*
kaufen.

Er verhält sich, als **sei** er *He behaves as if he were the*
der Chef.   *boss.*

This index lists key words in German and English as well as grammatical terms. Many references are included under several different headings. For example:

- you can locate information on the German definite article by looking up 'articles, definite', 'definite article' or 'der, die, das';
- you can find out whether a verb forms its perfect tense with **sein** by referring to 'perfect tense', 'tenses' or '**sein**';
- you can check the comparative form of the adjective **gut** by looking up '**gut**', or by looking under 'adjectives, comparative' or 'comparative adjectives/adverbs'.